EFFECTIVE MATHS TEACHING

Also published by Stanley Thornes (Publishers) Ltd:

D.P. Brown & R. Nacino-Brown   *Effective Teaching Practice*
D. Frith & H.G. Macintosh   *A Teacher's Guide to Assessment*
L. Walklin   *Instructional Techniques and Practice*
L. Walklin   *Teaching and Learning in Further and Adult Education*

EFFECTIVE MATHS TEACHING

A Guide to
Teaching Basic Mathematical Concepts

John Busbridge and David Womack

Stanley Thornes (Publishers) Ltd

First published in 1991 by:
Stanley Thornes (Publishers) Ltd
Old Station Drive
Leckhampton
CHELTENHAM GI53 0DN
England

British Library Cataloguing in Publication Data

Busbridge, John
    Effective maths teaching: A guide to teaching
    basic mathematical concepts.
    I. Title   II. Womack, David
    372.7

    ISBN 0-7487-1157-0

Typeset by Tech-Set, Gateshead, Tyne & Wear.
Printed and bound in Great Britain at The Bath Press, Avon.

Contents

Introduction

In the last thirty years there have been many changes in both the content and the style of mathematics teaching. Modern methods make greater demand for visual, physical aids to help children to understand concepts and processes. There is a need for all who teach young children to have a clear understanding of progression within the subject, and a wide range of resources and teaching strategies to help their pupils achieve mastery.

This book aims to equip both experienced teachers and students in training to make their mathematics classes stimulating and enjoyable. It gives suggestions for many effective learning aids which can be made using low-cost materials, and advocates, wherever possible, a practical activity-based methodology. The authors are familiar with the over-crowded and under-resourced conditions in which many teachers and children have to work, but believe that it is possible to teach mathematics using such methods and materials in spite of those constraints. Their experience in working with Primary teachers, advisers and inspectors in Africa has shown that the approach adopted in this book, and the making and use of the learning resources described, meet with a ready, enthusiastic response and fulfil a great need.

The Primary mathematics curriculum can be broadly divided under the headings of number, measure and shape; different chapters concern themselves with these separate branches, for each of which there is emphasis on a clear, logical progression of work with the stages of development clearly defined. The inclusion of photographs of many of the learning aids should convince the reader that their making is feasible; in every case the materials required are readily available as waste or at very low cost.

CHAPTER ONE

Teaching, Planning and Assessment

1.1 LEARNING AND TEACHING

The teaching of mathematics has undergone many changes in the last 100 years. Fifty years ago, it was for the most part taught very formally. The teacher explained a rule on the blackboard, gave some examples of the rule in operation, and then set the class many more examples and exercises to do for themselves. Teachers believed that understanding would eventually come through sufficient practice.

This philosophy of mathematics teaching was questioned when psychologists began to study how children see the world around them. Investigations were made, by the Swiss-born researcher Jean Piaget and others, into how and why children come to understand mathematical concepts. Mathematics teaching today has taken account of this research and now follows the way children learn, rather than what may be described as a more 'logical' development of a topic. This is what we mean by *child-centred* education.

American educational philosophy has developed in a rather different way towards a more structured approach to teaching, stressing *behavioural objectives* for each lesson or topic. These objectives are carefully planned so that the teacher can measure how far they have been achieved at the end of each lesson or period of time. This approach, sometimes known as *direct instruction*, has been particularly successful in Special Education.

1.11 Understanding concepts

Today's teachers find themselves influenced by both these philosophies and it is sometimes difficult to decide whether a discovery approach or direct instructional approach should be adopted. In general, a closely structured approach is suitable when children are learning a rule or mathematical procedure. However, when introducing a concept, the

1

teacher should try to guide the children to discover and understand the idea for themselves. In order to do this, it may be necessary to lead them through a series of stages in forming the concept.

Mathematical concepts are the central ideas behind a mathematical topic, for example, place value, the idea of a fraction splitting a whole into a number of equal parts or conservation of number. It is only through the use of many different examples and materials that a child can eventually abstract a concept from the learning situation. Ideally, these learning situations should be 'concrete'. For example, place value can be introduced through bundles of ten sticks, ten-strips or the place-value abacus (see Chapter 3). It is advisable to introduce only one new concept at a time to ensure that it is firmly grasped before moving on to a new idea. If the teacher knows a concept to be difficult, then he or she should prepare for it as carefully as possible using suitable examples and materials. Wrong ideas, once implanted, may take a long time to be replaced by correct ones.

1.12 Teaching topics

A topic may involve several difficult concepts or no new concepts at all. For example, addition of fractions with the same denominator ($\frac{1}{5} + \frac{3}{5}$), may not involve any concepts other than those already understood (i.e. addition of like items such as one orange plus three oranges, etc). When teaching a new topic, the teacher should relate it to what the child already knows, building on ideas which are already understood.

Efficient learning requires the learner to be motivated and interested in the topic. Therefore, the same topic should not be taught for too long but, where possible, should be broken up into sections. Teachers should ensure also that there is a variety in the mode of activities for the pupil to do; for example, some listening, some writing, reading or drawing. When a pupil seems to be experiencing real difficulty with a topic, give plenty of praise and encouragement for correct work. A certain amount of repetition may be necessary in such cases, but try to repeat the same idea in a slightly different way. If a pupil cannot grasp an idea introduced in one way, look for another way of presenting the same idea – perhaps, using a different learning medium or a carefully prepared learning aid.

1.13 Organising work

Worked examples are useful in the teaching situation, but these should be graded in order of difficulty. It is better to take a longer but more certain path than to cut corners and so confuse the child.

Worksheets   are a convenient means of grading the more difficult sections of arithmetic, such as regrouping or the decomposition method of subtraction (see Chapter 3).

Oral questioning   is an effective means both of teaching and of testing whether pupils have understood a topic. However, such evaluation will only be reliable if the teacher addresses the questions to individual pupils, preferably by name. An undirected question may provoke a chorus answer which is usually no more than an attempt to please the teacher ; class answering is often dominated by the more able pupils. Be sure to direct some questions to the less able or naturally quieter individuals. In this way the teacher can discover whether those pupils have understood the teaching. Such questions should be prepared when planning the lesson beforehand and should aim to bring out the particular points which the teacher wishes to make. At all times, *encourage children to ask questions* and be prepared to spend some time answering them.

1.2 PLANNING A SCHEME OF WORK

Before planning a scheme of work for mathematics, the headteacher should consult with those responsible for administering the scheme. The scheme should have as its basis, a set of aims or objectives which will be achieved if the scheme is taught well and, once decided upon, should be made known to all members of staff. Some aims will relate to the whole of the mathematics curriculum while others may be concerned only with a particular area of mathematics. For example, the aims for measurement in the lower Primary classes may be tabulated in a chart such as Fig. 1.1 (overleaf). This may be used to assess the progress of the whole class or for individual pupils. When each item has been successfully carried out, the appropriate line can be ticked.

As a further example, we can consider objectives which might be set for young children learning to count for the first time. Objectives are generally shorter term and more specific than aims. Their attainment can usually be measured and may be recorded in a chart such as Fig. 1.2 (page 5). This chart records, for each of the numbers 1 to 10, six different (though related) tasks which show the child's understanding of the numerals used in counting.

USING NON-STANDARD UNITS

Can a pupil measure:
Length: How long is an item (e.g. measured in hand-spans)? _____
Weight: How much does an item weigh (e.g. measured in beads)? _____

Volume: How much does a container hold (e.g. measured in cupfuls)? _____

Time: How long does an activity take (e.g. measured in pendulum swings)? _____

ASSESSING PRACTICAL SKILLS

Can a pupil measure (in standard units):
Length: The length of an item (in cm or m)? _____
Weight: The weight of an item (in g or kg)? _____
Volume: The volume of a liquid (in litres)? _____
Time: The length of time an activity takes (in minutes)? _____

Can a pupil:
Length: Use centimetre and metre rules to measure out a stated length? _____
Weight: Use gram and kilogram weights to weigh out a stated quantity? _____
Volume: Pour out a stated volume of liquid? _____
Time: Time an event (in minutes and seconds)? _____

KNOWLEDGE OF UNITS

Does a pupil know:
Length: Number of cm in 1 metre? _____
                     metres in 1 km? _____
Weight: Number of g in 1 kg? _____
                     kg in 1 tonne? _____
Volume: Number of ml in 1 litre? _____
Time: Number of hours in 1 day? _____
                     days in 1 week? _____
          Number of months in 1 year? _____
                     minutes in 1 hour? _____
          Number of seconds in 1 minute? _____
                     days in 1 month? _____

Fig. 1.1   Aims for measurement – lower Primary

1.21 Checklist for numbers 1 to 10

Children need to write and recognise the numerals (number symbols) from 0 to 9. They need also to count collections of objects and count out a given number of objects from a larger collection using the chart. Teachers can note the following information for any pupil in the class.

Name												Year: Class:
Item presented by teacher to pupil	*Required pupil's response*	1	2	3	4	5	6	7	8	9	10	
Objects to count	Count objects and say numeral											
Objects to count	Count objects and write numeral											
Spoken numeral	Count out that number of objects											
Written numeral	Count out that number of objects											
Spoken numeral	Write the numeral											
Written numeral	Say the numeral											

Fig. 1.2   Checklist for numbers 1 to 10

Can the pupil:

1 Count a given collection of objects and *say* how many there are?

2 Count a given collection of objects and *write down* how many there are?

3 Given a *spoken* numeral, count out the appropriate number of objects?

4 Given a *written* numeral, count out the appropriate number of objects?

5 Write down a *spoken* numeral?

6 Read a *written* numeral?

(Note that knowledge of the *written* numeral words ('six', etc.) is not asked for here.) A tick in the appropriate section will indicate a child's success in each activity.

For example, for the number 4, the teacher can sit with a pupil and a tray of shells, a piece of paper and pencil. The six activities would then take the form:

1 Teacher gives pupil four shells to count. Pupil counts them and says, 'Four'.

2 Teacher gives pupil four shells to count. Pupil counts them and writes '4'.

3 Teacher tells pupil, 'Count out four shells.' Pupil counts out four shells.

4 Teacher tells pupil, 'Count out this number of shells,' and shows numeral 4 on a card. Pupil counts out four shells.

5 Teacher tells pupil, 'Write down four.' Pupil writes down the numeral '4'.

6 Teacher says to pupil, 'Tell me what is this number,' and shows numeral 4 on a card. Pupil says, 'Four'.

Using this record sheet, a profile of a child's strengths and weaknesses in the six different tasks can be obtained.

1.3 EVALUATION

1.31 Testing for attainment of objectives

Before setting a test, the teacher must decide which skills and concepts the class should have mastered. These will generally be the objectives listed in the scheme of work for the class. As an example, the objectives for pupils to achieve might be:

1 Subtract one two-digit number from another, with decomposition, setting out the computation in vertical form.

2 Measure the length of a line segment to an accuracy of 0.1 cm.

3 Construct a triangle given the lengths of all three sides.

Such skills and knowledge can be tested precisely by setting items such as the following:

1 Subtract 37 from 82 (*set your working out clearly*).

2 Measure the length of this line *to the nearest millimetre.*

3 Construct a triangle with side lengths 3 cm, 5 cm and 6 cm *using ruler and compasses; show your method of construction clearly.*

Notice how important the italicised words are, if the pupil responses are to be assessed fairly.

1.32 Testing knowledge of the syllabus

A test may be given to find out whether the pupil has learnt the basics of the syllabus taught so far. The questions should cover all the sections and topics taught in equal proportions. For example, if 50 per cent of the marks in a test are awarded for questions covering only 10 per cent of the topics being tested, then obviously the test is a poor one with respect to the purpose for which it was made. Test items should be kept simple and uncomplicated since, if the answer to the question involves several different steps and techniques, it may be very difficult to assess where the pupil has made an error. The questions should be worded in a way which is familiar to pupils and the time allowed should be generous.

1.33 Testing for ability

On the other hand, a test may be given to find out which pupils in the class show most potential for further work in mathematics or which pupils are more able to deal with a wide range of problems. In this case, the questions could require pupils to choose which process or method to use. Questions may be worded in ways that have not been met before and there should be a strict time limit which may not allow all the pupils to finish the test.

1.34 Record-keeping

Record-keeping may be carried out to provide information for the teacher or for the headteacher. Its purpose may be to show which parts of the syllabus have been covered so far or which objectives pupils have attained. Records may also be kept of the results of a number of short tests to remind the teacher which parts of the syllabus may require further revision.

In arithmetic, it is important to know how far pupils have progressed in their understanding of the main stages of the algorithms. An example of a very simple but effective form of record-keeping is shown in Fig. 1.3 (overleaf).

Class: Teacher: Year:	Pupils' Names												
	Juma												
Numbers 1–10 Numerals Checklist	✓												
Addition +	✓												
Subtraction −	✓												
Multiplication ×													
Division ÷													
Numbers 0–100 Numerals													
+ No regrouping													
+ Regrouping													
− No regrouping													
− Regrouping													
× No regrouping													
× Regrouping													
÷ No regrouping													
÷ Regrouping													

Fig. 1.3   Arithmetic checklist

This can be an indication to the (head)teacher of what stage the class has reached. It also records individual attainment in arithmetic for each child in the class, showing which children may be falling behind in subtraction, division, etc. For example, the chart shows that Juma knows the numerals 1 to 10 as tested by the checklist (Fig. 1.3), and simple addition and subtraction but has not yet mastered multiplication and division.

1.35 Diagnosis

A pupil or group of pupils may be experiencing particular difficulty with a mathematical concept or topic such as subtraction. In this case the teacher may need to see such pupils individually or in a small group and should ask questions appropriate to the area of difficulty to check exactly where the problem arises. For example, a pupil may consistently fail to get the correct answer in using the multiplication algorithm. The problem may lie in lack of knowledge of multiplication facts, or in the wrong alignment of figures, or in errors with 'carrying'. The teacher can only discover this with certainty if he observes the pupil working out such problems. He may notice that the pupil is using a multiplication chart incorrectly or using his fingers and miscounting. Such observation is known as *diagnostic assessment*. Although this is very time-consuming it may well save much more time later on, since a wrong practice learnt only results in compounding the problem at a later stage.

1.4 LEARNING AND TEACHING AIDS

Teaching aids are just that – aids to teaching. The aim of all teaching is that the child should learn and therefore we could more accurately call such teaching aids *learning aids*. Learning aids do not replace the need for good teaching, but supplement it.

Charts which summarise a rule are not ideal teaching aids since they do not require the presence or aid of a teacher, although they may help pupils to learn a rule. However, a good teaching aid is a piece of apparatus which can be used by the teacher and pupils to demonstrate or explain a mathematical idea. For example, number strips used with a number track (see Chapter 3) help children to recognise the unchanging order of numbers, so that to solve $15 + 4$,   it is not necessary to collect 15 objects and 4 objects and count the total; we can just add 4 to the number 15 on the track.

All the learning aids suggested in this book can be made from simple, cheap materials which are easy to obtain. These are usually 'junk' items which have been discarded, such as empty food packets and tins, old newspapers and plastic oil containers. Any stationery required is limited to paper clips, paper, card and glue, etc. The pupils themselves can be asked to bring these along to school, but try to work with clean material.

Some of the learning aids described here can be made individually by the pupils themselves and taken home, such as a set of numeral cards (see Chapter 2). Others should be kept safely by the teacher and only brought out when their use is required. To leave apparatus around which is not being used serves no useful purpose.

Whether the teacher uses the aid to demonstrate to the whole class or pupils use it themselves in small groups depends on the size of the class and the teacher's ability to organise group work. However, the old Chinese proverb is still as relevant today as when it was first uttered :

I hear and I forget; I see and I remember; I do *and I understand.*

CHAPTER TWO

First Experiences with Numbers

2.1 PRE-PRIMARY ACTIVITIES

Children learn from their surroundings. Most children are naturally curious and will benefit greatly from a stimulating and interesting home environment. Parents should therefore try to save clean, empty food packets, tins, bottle tops and other items which can eventually be used by young children for counting or measuring. However, children must be given the chance to investigate freely by touching, pulling, stretching or bending since these are a child's attempts to find the size, weight and other properties of an object.

There are many pre-school situations in which children can develop their first mathematical concepts; some of these are now listed.

2.11 Exploring a plot of land

Children can discover and count the different kinds of plants and insects in a plot of land. They can observe how quickly the plants grow and watch how fast a beetle moves. Children should be encouraged to use mathematical words to describe the movement of insects –*forwards, backwards, left, right, under, over, around, in, out,* etc. As they do so, they are learning mathematical concepts. When they notice the change in height as plants grow they are comparing sizes; this is the beginning of measurement. They can collect different leaves, grasses and seeds, noting the longest, largest, heaviest or smallest. These can later be sorted into those of the same kind or ordered according to length or weight. These ideas soon lead to sorting and ordering numbers and so to the start of mathematics.

2.12 Play with sand and water

Through play with sand and water, children meet the mathematical concepts of volume, capacity and weight. Parents and teachers should provide milk cartons, plastic bottles, tin cans, funnels, tubes and sponges. Children can then fill one container with sand or water and pour the contents into another container.

When they pour sand into a vessel of a different shape, children will learn that the quantity of water or sand remains the same whatever the appearance and shape of the vessel holding it. This is the mathematical principle of *conservation*.

Children should play at filling one container from another, and so discover, for example, how many full milk cartons will fill a bucket.

Words such as *more, less, most, heavy, light, plenty, once, twice,* etc., should be used correctly by the teacher when they are needed.

2.13 Travelling by road

When travelling, children may see many different geometrical shapes, for example, the circular wheels of cars, cylindrical petrol-tankers, triangular electricity pylons, etc. Car number-plate numbers can be spotted and games played, such as looking for the numbers 1 to 9 in sequence. Travelling also gives older children the opportunity to make estimates of time and distance, and eventually to relate these to places on a map.

2.14 Shopping

Shopping gives valuable mathematical experience when numbers, shapes and measures of all kinds are pointed out. When buying clothes, children's attention should be drawn to questions about body measurement :

How tall are you ?
How long are the sleeves ?, etc.

This shows the *need* for measurement. Children should be allowed to buy simple items from nearby shops and see the money clearly counted out.

2.15 Collecting

Children enjoy collecting all sorts of objects of the same kind – bottle tops, beans, seeds, flowers, etc. These objects can later be used for sorting, ordering and matching activities. As children grow older these important classifying and sorting activities may become more sophisticated, e.g. doing jigsaws, collecting stamps, listing the names of all known animals, etc.

2.16   Questions about time

Questions should be asked such as:

How long is it to your birthday?
How many days?
How old will you be then?
How many days' holiday do we have?
What time is breakfast?
What time is dinner?

Question children about the times of radio or television programmes and other habitual routines. This involves estimating durations of time and makes children eager to learn how to tell the time.

2.17   Traditional stories

Each local culture has its own collection of children's stories, many involving numbers. Some English language fairy tales are well known in many different cultures, for example, *Snow White and the Seven Dwarfs*, *Goldilocks and the Three Bears*, and others. These introduce numbers and comparisons in a pleasant and enjoyable context for young children.

2.2   LANGUAGE AND VOCABULARY

Language helps to fix mathematical concepts in children's minds. Teachers should introduce the words in the following lists at appropriate times according to the development of the child. The word should always be introduced for the first time in a practical and realistic situation. A word should *not* be used for the first time to refer to a situation which is not present to the child. For example, to introduce the word 'big' say, 'This book is big', and not, 'My father is big'. If a word is used in the right way at the right time, then children will learn both to *understand* and to *use* it correctly.

These lists are of increasing difficulty.

List 1

big, small, long, short, great, large, tiny, hot, cold, fat, thin, high, low, time, day, night, once, twice, first, second, beginning, end, now, then, near, far, up, down, in, out, front, back, here, there.

List 2

broad, wide, narrow, tall, short, under, over, above, below, quick, slow, before, after, soon, late, early, morning, afternoon, evening, middle, between, whole, part, plenty, few, many, lot more, less, equal, greater than, less than, more than, fewer than, more, altogether.

Comparatives: bigger, smaller, heavier, lighter, higher, lower, etc. (see List 1).

List 3

when, where, until, all, some, none, double, treble (triple), halve, how long, how short, how near, how far, hollow, solid, amount, cost, price, size.

Superlatives: biggest, smallest, heaviest, etc.

Fraction words: half, quarter, third, etc.

List 4   Essential logical words

and, not, or, but, true, false.

Harder words: therefore, because, although, neither . . . nor, if . . . then, (e.g. If I drop the egg, then it will break).

Use vernacular (local) words to help to explain the meaning of these words if necessary.

There are many more special mathematical words which pupils will meet at later stages: number words such as *fraction, remainder, multiply*, etc., measurement words such as *perimeter, volume, right angle*, etc., shape words such as *parallelogram, sector, sphere*, etc., and general words such as *average, scale, graph*, etc. These should be introduced only when the topic is taught but teachers should check that the words are explained and understood by *all* the pupils in the class.

2.3 PRE-NUMBER EXPERIENCES

Pre-number experiences form an important basis for the mathematical thinking children need in their first few years at school. For example, before children can begin to count they will need to recognise the difference between, say, a collection of *four* objects and a collection of *five* objects. Groups of four have different properties from groups of five and children should discover these differences by sorting, arranging in order of size or in patterns and by matching the objects in different collections.

Through the activities described in this section, children will learn to observe, compare and discriminate. The skills they develop through such activities will lead them to accurate and meaningful counting and so to an understanding of number.

2.31 **Preparing for class activities**

Teachers should collect a wide range of simple objects for children to use freely in the classroom. The pupils themselves can be asked to help in this. These simple pre-number materials include: beans, seeds, sticks, grasses, leaves, buttons, tin lids, matchboxes, etc. Later, teachers might provide pictures from magazines or newspapers or make up their own by drawing on small cards.

The following activities are best carried out by a small group of children. The class can be split into several of these small groups. One group can be sorting, another ordering and others, matching. The teacher should walk round helping children to understand what they are doing.

2.32 **Sorting activities**

Children should classify objects according to different properties or criteria; for example, sort objects by their *colour*, by their *shape*, by their *size*, by their *texture*.

Sorting bottle tops

A large number of mineral water (soda) bottle tops which show various brand names or flavours can be sorted into separate piles of lemonade, orangeade, tonic water, etc.

Sorting beans

A similar activity can be carried out with different kinds of bean.

Making a sorting tray

Four strong cartons can be stapled together in rows of two to form a tray. This can be used to separate the different items being sorted. A slightly higher ridge in one direction will provide a convenient tray for the next activity.

A harder exercise: sorting by two attributes (properties)

A number of small rectangles and triangles can be cut from the back of a cardboard carton. A similar number can be cut from another piece of card, of a different colour (or the same card can be coloured) to provide a set of rectangles and triangles of a different colour. If these colours are red and blue, then ask children to:

1 Sort the triangles from the squares.

2 Sort the red shapes from the blue shapes.

3 Sort all the shapes into four piles on the desk.

This is sorting by two *attributes* or *properties*, colour and shape, at the same time.

2.33   Ordering activities

Make a collection of small straight sticks of differing lengths. Ask children to arrange these in order of size from the shortest to the longest. Begin by using three or four sticks, then progress gradually to ten sticks or more.

A similar activity can be carried out with circular tin lids or cartons.

2.34   Matching activities

In these activities no counting is to take place. Collections of objects are compared only by matching objects from one group with objects from another.

Matching beans and bottle tops

Give children two sets of objects, e.g. beans and bottle tops. Ask them, 'Are there more beans or more bottle tops?'

To answer this, the children need to pair them off, each pair consisting of one bean and one bottle top. At the end, there may be some beans unpaired, so there are more beans than bottle tops. The *number* of beans is *more than* the *number* of bottle tops. If the pairing matches the beans and bottle tops exactly, then there are the *same number* of beans and bottle tops; the number of beans and bottle tops are *equal*.

At this stage no number words need be used; the children are only finding out which collection has *more* objects. The numbers of objects which children handle should gradually increase from about six to twelve or more. Activities can be extended to collections of three different kinds.

Matching activities using pupils

Match a group of girls to a group of boys so that each has a partner. Are there any girls/boys left over?

Match a collection of books to a set of girls.

Match a collection of chairs to a set of boys.

Match a collection of milk cartons to a set of children.

Matching activities using picture cards

After children have matched object with object, they will be able to match with pictures.

1 Children can be shown pictures which contain a mixture of two different kinds of object; for example, mangoes and bananas or men and women. Are there more mangoes than bananas or more men than women? Children can find out by pairing each mango with a banana with a light pencil line.

2 The teacher can make, by drawing, sets of cards for children to sort. Make about ten copies of each picture card. Then give children, for example, eight pictures of a hen and ten pictures of an egg. After matching correctly there will be two pictures of eggs left over. Alternatively, give out all the picture cards and ask children to match the pairs of cards which go together.

2.4 COUNTING

Counting is using a sequence of words (one, two, three, . . .) to correspond with the items to be counted. These items may be beans, steps taken or even the chimes of a bell.

2.41 Understanding counting

In order to count, a child must:

1 Know the conventional sequence of number names 'one, two, three, . . .'. These are the *cardinal* numbers.

2 Be able to match these words 'one-by-one' to the objects being counted: *one-to-one correspondence*.

3 Understand that the last word in a count gives the numerical size of the collection of objects counted. (This is the *cardinality* of the collection.)

Note, there are two different counting situations with which the child should be familiar: *counting* and *counting out*.

Counting means to count every object in a given collection. The number of objects is only found after counting.

Counting out means to count a stated number of objects by separating them from a larger collection. In this case, the child is told the number of objects to be counted out and stops counting when he or she has reached that number.

A child who really understands what it means to count to ten, should be able:

1 To state in words the numerical size of any collection of objects up to ten.

2 To write down as a numeral, the size of any collection up to ten.

3 When given a spoken numeral up to ten, to count out that number of objects.

4 When given a written numeral up to ten, to count out that number of objects.

5 To read and state correctly, any numeral up to ten written down by the teacher.

6 To write down any numeral up to ten which is spoken by the teacher.

2.42 Errors in counting

Here are some of the more common errors that children make when first learning to count:

1 Pupils count the same object twice, or omit to count one of the objects.
   Remedy   Arrange the objects to be counted in a line, well spread out. Ask the child to count them. Next arrange the objects in a wide circle and have the child count them again. Then make the circle smaller and let the child again count them. Finally, scatter the objects in a random pattern and let the child count them.

   More generally, any one-to-one correspondence activities will be appropriate (see Section 2.3).

2 Pupils miss out one of the number names or confuse the order, e.g. . . . 345689 . . . or . . . 3457689 . . .
   Remedy   Teach the children to say a number nursery rhyme or ask the class to repeat the order of numbers aloud.

3 Pupils do not make the number word sequence 1, 2, 3, . . . correspond with the objects being counted.
   Remedy   Ask the child to pick up each object in turn before saying each number word. The teacher can then say the correct number name with the child. Alternatively, make children clap their hands as they say the number names. This is useful as a general class activity.

2.5 WRITING THE NUMERALS

Numerals are the symbols used to write numbers; for example, the number 573 (five hundred and seventy-three) uses three numerals (5, 7 and 3).

The written numerals we use are 1, 2, 3, 4, 5, 6, 7, 8, 9, 0. We call these *digits*.

The written number words are *one*, *two*, *three*, *four*, . . . The spoken numerals are these words spoken out aloud, 'one', 'two', 'three', 'four', . . .

Note   In some countries, 1 is used for 1 and 7 for 7. Also, on a computer keyboard and screen Ø or θ is sometimes used for zero.

2.51 **Writing activities**

Make sure that pupils begin writing numerals in a correct way; it is difficult later to unlearn wrong habits. Here are some simple ideas to help children to write the numerals correctly.

1 Use dots to show the correct starting point and arrows to show the direction the child's pencil should take (see Fig. 2.1).

Fig. 2.1

2 Cut out templates from card for the child to draw around (see Fig. 2.2).

Draw *round* this template

Draw *inside* this template

Fig. 2.2   a)   b)

The numeral, Fig. 2.2a, can be felt when held behind the back. Template Fig. 2.2b can be drawn inside.

3 Ask the child to trace the shape of the numeral in the air, or in sand. Stand behind the child to show the correct way.

4 Make the children repeat to themselves exactly what they are doing as they each write the numeral.
   For example, for the numeral 7, 'go across then down', etc.

5 Let children draw the numerals on the blackboard.

Note A left-handed child writes towards the right hand which holds the paper or book steady; this can cause difficulties not encountered by right-handed children.

2.6 CARDINAL NUMBERS

2.61 Class activities to teach the cardinal numbers

Using a set of number boxes

Cut a set of ten strong cardboard cartons (UHT milk cartons are ideal) in the shape shown in Fig. 2.3 and fasten them together with sticky tape, glue or staples. Label the back wall of each box with the numerals 1 to 10.

Fig. 2.3

Various sets of items can be simply made by the teacher for the child to place into the appropriate sections of the boxes. These items can include the following:

Bundles of one to ten sticks,
Sets of cards on which are drawn one to ten objects,
Sets of cards of different marked lengths,
Sets of cards with holes punched into them,
Sets of bottle tops on string.

Several sets of each type may be made to give children plenty of practice in finding the right compartment for each item. The child will need to count in order to place the larger number sets correctly.

Using a set of matchboxes

In separate open matchboxes place a number of beans for each of the numbers one to ten. Label each of the matchboxes with the numerals 1 to 10.

1 Give a matchbox to a child. Ask, 'How many beans are in the box ?'.

2 Give a child an empty matchbox, labelled with '5'. Ask, 'Can you put five beans in the box ?'.

3 Ask a child to find the box with four beans in it, etc.

Using a set of numeral cards

Write the numerals 1 to 10 on a plain piece of card or on paper stuck on to (used) card. Cut these up and use them separately, or thread them on a piece of string, and hang them on the classroom wall. Pictures of the appropriate number of objects can be stuck on the back of the cards. If the teacher wants to display the numerals but also have them readily available for pupils' use, then paper clips can be used to attach the cards to the string.

1 Ask the child to hand you a numeral. For example, teacher asks, 'Give me the number six'.

2 Point to one of the numerals. Ask the child to tell you which number it is.

3 Give the child any three numerals. Ask him or her to put them in order starting from the lowest number.

4 Using also the set of matchboxes described above, ask the pupils to :

Arrange the correct numerals beside the appropriate boxes.
Put the correct number of beans in the boxes beside the numerals.

Bottle tops on string

Bottle tops can be threaded on lengths of string to make a set of strings holding from one to ten tops. Tie knots in the string to separate the bottle tops ; attach labels to each string to show the number of tops. The set of strings can then be displayed on the classroom wall.

Similar sets of number strings can be made using rectangles of cardboard, paper butterflies or merely large overhand bow knots in the string.

1 Ask children to put the strings in order of numerical size with the '1' string on the left.

2 Use activities similar to those with matchboxes (see above).

Odd and even cards

These can be made from cardboard marked into squares of side 2 cm or 3 cm and cut out in the patterns shown in Fig. 2.4. The appropriate numeral can be written on the reverse of each card. Children can arrange the ten cards in order of size using either side of the cards.

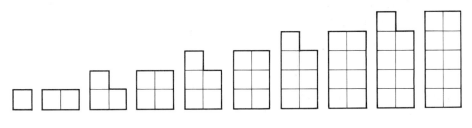

Fig. 2.4

The cards show the *odd* and *even* numbers by the projecting square on the odd numbers. They also show that an odd number plus an odd number always makes an even number.

Nursery rhymes

Children can learn the sequence of number names through nursery rhymes such as:

One, two, this is my shoe
Three, four, shut the door
Five, six, a bundle of sticks
Seven, eight, a big white plate
Nine, ten, say it again

and other local rhymes.

Counting activities involving pupils

1 Ask a number of pupils to come to the front of the class. The teacher asks, 'How many children are here?'

2 With the same group of children the teacher may ask, 'How many legs are here altogether?', 'How many eyes?', etc.

3 Two children come to the front of the class. Each holds up a certain number of fingers that they choose. Teacher asks, 'How many fingers are held up altogether?' (Alternatively, the teacher can do this.)

4 Ask an active pupil to jump up and down in front of the class while the class counts the jumps.

5 Count miscellaneous objects in boxes.

Zig-zag cards

Make a set of ten cards (see Fig. 2.5). Cut each of these into two pieces in a zig-zag fashion, but differently for each card. Jumble all the pieces up and ask pupils to fit them together again.

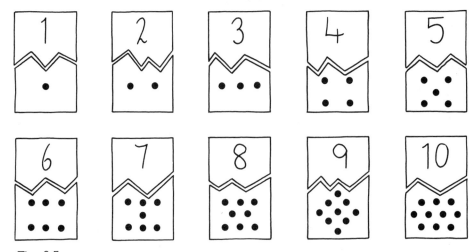

Fig. 2.5

Zig-zag cards can also be made with pictures of objects instead of dots.

Game of snap

Make several sets of cards, each card containing a number of dots from one to ten or the numerals one to ten. Share the cards between two or more players, who arrange their cards face down in a pile before them. Each player takes a turn to place one of his cards on a central stack. If the card being placed represents the same number as the card already on top of the stack, then the first player to call 'snap' takes all the cards in the stack. The first player to lose all his cards is the loser.

Hopscotch

The numbers 1–10 are drawn in squares on the ground. Children take turns to throw a small stone on to square 1. The child must hop *over* that square into square 2 and then on to square 3, etc., until the last square is reached. The stone is then thrown on to square 2 and the child must hop

over this, from square 1 to square 3 and then on to square 4, and so on.
Play continues until the child has thrown the stone on to all the squares
in sequence. A mistake in the hopping, or inaccurate throwing, sends the
child to the back of the queue.

Tossing pebbles

Two pupils take turns to toss pebbles into two boxes, or rectangles,
drawn on the floor of the classroom. Points are gained for each pebble
which lands in the correct box. If a pebble lands in an opponent's box then
the opponent gains that point.

Match point

One child picks up a number of cleaned used matches in one hand. The
other player has to guess how many are hidden. If the guessing player
guesses correctly, he or she keeps a match to one side, has a turn to scoop
up a number of matches and the first player must guess. A single match
is taken for each correct guess. The first player to gain ten matches (ten
correct guesses) is the winner.

2.62   Conservation of number

A child counts a line of pebbles ; first he counts in one direction from end
to end, and reaches the number ten. Then he counts the pebbles in the
opposite direction and again reaches ten. By counting them when they
are arranged in a circle, or in different patterns the child discovers that
he *always* reaches ten. He has discovered that the number of pebbles is
conserved, whatever the arrangement or however he counts them.

The importance of this concept of *conservation of number* in a child's
development was first shown by the Swiss psychologist Jean Piaget. He
devised tests for children, to determine whether they had grasped the
concept or not. For example, young children do not at first realise that
the number of beans in a line remains the same when they are spread out
so that it looks as if there are more.

Ensure that children have discovered conservation for themselves
before beginning any introduction to arithmetic. Teachers should not
tell children, but should give plenty of experience of rearranging a
number of counters in different ways and patterns and letting children
count them each time. Fig. 2.6 shows five different patterns for seven
counters. It is not sufficient to teach each number from a single pattern
of dots on a wall-chart or teaching aid.

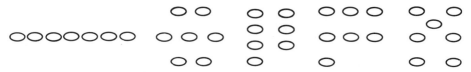

Fig. 2.6

If the same counters are rearranged in different ways, does the child know that there *must* be the same number each time?

Activities

1 Ask children to count a collection of objects in several different ways.

2 Split a group of objects into two boxes and ask children to count and record the total. Divide the objects among the two boxes in a different way and again ask the children to record the total.

3 Ask children to arrange six beans, for example, in as many different ways as they can.

2.7 ORDINAL NUMBERS

'First', 'second', 'third', . . . are known as the *ordinal* numbers. This distinguishes them from the cardinal number names 'one', 'two', 'three', . . . A cardinal number describes the *size* of a collection of objects; the ordinal number describes the *position* of a single item in that collection. Both these aspects of number are involved in counting. For example, pointing to the sixth tree in a line of trees means there are six trees altogether up to that point. The ordinal number of an object in a group indicates the size (cardinal number) of the group which has so far been counted.

2.71 Class activities to teach the ordinal numbers

1 Ask the child to count ordinally (first, second, third, . . .) the following sequence of events and actions:
Tapping of a ruler or percussion instrument
The steps taken by a child
Bouncing of a ball
Number of skips with a skipping rope
Banging two pebbles together
Running around a circular course
Rings of a bell.

2 Ask the child to count ordinally the following objects:
   Fingers of the hand from left to right (fingers always keep the same relative positions, the thumb being 'first')
   Books standing on a shelf
   Soda bottles standing in a line
   Bottle tops or beads threaded on a string
   Beans as they are dropped into a tin held by the child. (Here the child is using his senses of sight, sound and touch.)

3 Ask the children to draw a picture each day starting on Monday and writing '1st picture', '2nd picture', etc. Count the number of pictures at the end of the week.

4 Give children successive ordinal numbers as they arrive in the classroom in the morning; give ordinal positions to the children in a race. Later ask the children to arrange themselves into lines in that order.

5 Arrange children in order of height (see Fig. 2.7) or weight, size of family, etc.

Fig 2.7

6 Ask children to recall a sequence of events or experiences, e.g. 'Tell me what you did when you got up this morning.'
'First I put on my sandals, . . .'

7 Make children follow instructions :

The 1st thing you do is trace over the picture.
The 2nd thing you do is . . .

8 Worksheets. Fig. 2.8 shows two typical examples which can be duplicated.

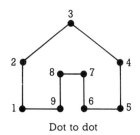

Dot to dot

Start from the bus marked ∗ and colour the third bus green.

Fig. 2.8   a)   b)

2.8 ZERO

Zero occupies a special place in our number system. It is used to show the number of objects in an empty box, but it is also used as a 'place-holder' in large numbers, e.g. in 200, the zeros keep the 2 in the *hundreds* place, in 307, it shows there are no tens. It is generally best to introduce 0 to young children after they are familiar with the numbers 1 to 9.

2.9 EXERCISES

1 You have a large number of beans, of four different and distinct sizes. Describe two different activities which you could carry out using these beans.

2 Describe some material which you could design for sorting activities which involve three different attributes, e.g. colour, shape, size, etc.

3 Describe a piece of apparatus which you could make to test a first year Primary pupil's knowledge of any aspect of the numerals 1 to 9.

4 Zero may be introduced to children using 'counting down' rhymes or songs. Give examples of any of these which you know.

2.91 **Hints, suggestions and answers**

1 Sort by colour and shape; order by size; match one type to another, etc.
Generally, use any sorting, ordering or matching activity.

2 A set of cards could show, for example, three different *shapes* (circle, triangle,
square) in two clearly distinct *sizes* (large, small), and decorated with three
different *patterns* (stripes, dots, plain).

4 Here is a well-known English rhyme:

There are *ten* green bottles standing on the wall; (*repeat*)
But if *one* green bottle should accidentally fall
There'd be *nine* green bottles standing on the wall.
There are *nine* green bottles . . ., etc

Count down until:

There is *one* green bottle . . .
But if *that* green bottle . . .
There'd be *no* green bottles . . .

———————◆———————

CHAPTER THREE

Operations with Whole Numbers

3.1 INTRODUCTION

Arithmetic is largely concerned with combining pairs of numbers using the *operations* of addition, subtraction, multiplication and division. We add or multiply more than two numbers by working in steps, combining only two numbers at a time, e.g.

$$3 + 5 + 4 + 7 = 8 + 4 + 7 = 12 + 7 = 19$$

For this reason the operations are known as *binary* operations.

In teaching arithmetic, our aim is to enable pupils to perform these operations accurately and reasonably quickly. However, skill in arithmetic should not be achieved at the expense of understanding, otherwise pupils will not be able to apply their skills intelligently in appropriate situations.

Understanding will come initially through the young child's use of 'concrete' apparatus. As confidence is gained, the child's need for counting apparatus will decline; at this stage he or she should be encouraged to learn the basic facts, e.g.

$$3 + 5 = 8, \quad 4 \times 6 = 24, \text{ etc.},$$

by memory without requiring time to think out the answer. This knowledge, together with an understanding of the correct process or *algorithm*, will enable the pupil to carry through longer computation such as $327 + 1089$ or 214×23, etc.

Note that nowadays there is little value in making children carry out the algorithms with large numbers, such as $3078 \times 217\,935$, since the pocket-sized electronic calculator makes computation easier. However, children should be able to use algorithms confidently, in order to carry out realistic calculations such as those which arise in everyday commerce and living.

3.2 LEARNING AIDS FOR THE TEACHER TO MAKE

3.21 Demonstrating the facts of arithmetic

There are a number of aids which can help children greatly in learning the basic algorithms of arithmetic. All of these aids are simple to make and will cost the resourceful teacher nothing, since they consist mainly of cardboard cut from food containers. Good scissors, a straight-edged ruler and a clear marking pen will also be required. Sticky tape, a stapler and glue will undoubtedly improve the durability of some of the aids but are not essential. The abacus shown in Fig. 3.9 will require wood, nails and a hammer.

The number board and number track can be used early in arithmetic, and the place-value material in the later development of the algorithms.

A 1-to-100 number board with matching numeral cards

A chart with the numbers 1 to 100 prominently displayed is an important aid in any lower primary classroom. The chart can be made of cardboard and displayed on the wall. If large cardboard is not available, then a suitable size may be obtained by combining four smaller pieces of card to make up the whole chart, as shown in Fig. 3.1.

1	2	3	4	5	6	7	8	9	10
11	12	13	14	15	16	17	18	19	20
21	22	23	24	25	26	27	28	29	30
31	32	33	34	35	36	37	38	39	40
41	42	43	44	45	46	47	48	49	50
51	52	53	54	55	56	57	58	59	60
61	62	63	64	65	66	67	68	69	70
71	72	73	74	75	76	77	78	79	80
81	82	83	84	85	86	87	88	89	90
91	92	93	94	95	96	97	98	99	100

Fig. 3.1

This chart will serve as a classroom reference for demonstrating addition facts, such as

$$42 + 10 = 52,$$
$$52 + 10 = 62$$

These can be shown by noting the numbers in vertical columns. Subtraction facts can be shown in a similar way.

A smaller 1-to-100 number board (say, 50 cm × 50 cm) can be used on a desk with a set of numerals which fit on to the board. The one hundred cards required can be cut up from an identical board, marked out in a similar way.

The board and cards do not need to be square; any rectangle of cardboard is suitable, provided its length and breadth are each divided into ten equal parts.

Activities

With the chart alone

1 Using a stick to indicate each row on the chart, ask pupils to recite the numbers up to 100.

2 Ask individual pupils to recite the numbers between any two lines chosen by the teacher.

3 Let the class make their own copies of the chart on squared paper – preferably in their exercise books.

4 Draw part of the number square on the blackboard and demonstrate patterns of numbers to the whole class.

With cut-up numeral cards

1 Observe how long it takes the child to place all the numerals on the board in the correct order. This will show the child's familiarity with higher numbers and understanding of *tens* and *units*.

2 Give a certain sequence of numerals (say the numerals 60 to 70) to a child and ask him or her to arrange them in the correct order on the desk.

3 Give a collection of ten numeral cards chosen at random, to a child and let him or her arrange them in the correct order.

4 Turn the number board over, and ask children to arrange the cards in the correct order.

5 Give two numerals to each child in the class, and see whether each can come to the front and place the numerals correctly on the board.

A number track with accompanying number strips

The number track can extend from 1 to 20 or from 1 to 100 and is used for class counting and introducing simple arithmetic. Each number occupies an equal space along a cardboard track. Short sections of card can be joined together with sticky tape or glue to build up the track which can then be folded away when necessary.

Making number strips

These consist of thin strips of card on which are written numbers proportional to their length. They can be cut in 'staircase' fashion from a wider piece of cardboard as shown in Fig. 3.2. Several sets should be made in order to show repetition of a number.

1		9	
2		8	
3		7	
4		6	
5		5	

Fig. 3.2

If the number track is drawn on a wider piece of card, it can be folded-up to hold the number strips as shown in Fig. 3.3. The folded-up section should be secured at each end using sticky tape or staples to keep the track firm in use.

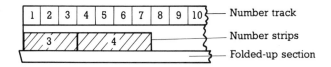

Fig. 3.3

Note that the number (length) can be written on one side of each strip. Fig. 3.3 shows the number track in use $(3 + 4 = 7)$.

The number line

A more 'advanced' number track is made up of points and can start from zero. This is known as a number line. Fig. 3.4 shows a number line from 1 to 100.

Fig. 3.4

The number line can eventually be 'filled in' to include the rational numbers (fractions) and extended 'backwards' to introduce the idea of negative numbers.

Note that a *track* uses spaces or boxes and starts from 1. A *line* uses points and can start from zero.

Activities

With the number track

Refer to the track or line for counting on and counting back. For example,

$$7 + 4 = 7, \ldots 8, \ldots 9, \ldots 10, \ldots 11 \qquad \boxed{7 \mid 8 \mid 9 \mid 10 \mid 11 \mid 12}$$

With the number strips alone:

1 Addition facts, e.g. $3 + 4 = 7$.

2 Subtraction facts, e.g. $6 - 2 = 4$.

3 Multiplication facts, e.g. $4 \times 2 = 8$.

4 Division facts, e.g. 6 shared between 3, or $6 \div 3$

With number track and number strips

1 Demonstrating addition and subtraction

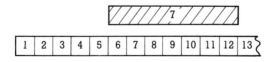

Fig. 3.5

Fig. 3.5 shows that $12 - 7 = 5$.

2 Demonstrating multiplication and division

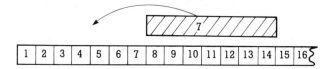

Fig. 3.6

Fig. 3.6 shows that $14 \div 7 = 2$ (repeated subtraction).

3.22   Demonstrating place-value

Place-value   is one of the most important concepts in arithmetic and one of the greatest sources of errors made by pupils. Place-value means that :

1 The value of a digit depends on its position.

2 The position denotes either 1's, 10's, 100's, ..., each position representing a power of ten (since we have ten different digits in our number system).

There are several different types of apparatus and activities which demonstrate this.

Place-value cards

These are sets of cards containing the numerals 1 to 9, the numerals 10 to 90 in multiples of 10, and the numerals 100 to 900 in multiples of 100, in the relative strip sizes shown in Fig. 3.7. They can be cut from several pieces of card, but one piece can be divided into 54 equal rectangles in order to cut out 9 units, 9 tens and 9 hundreds cards.

1	1	0	1	0	0
2	2	0	2	0	0
3	3	0	3	0	0
4	4	0	4	0	0
5	5	0	5	0	0
6	6	0	6	0	0
7	7	0	7	0	0
8	8	0	8	0	0
9	9	0	9	0	0

Fig. 3.7

Use three of these cards, one from each set, to make any number up to 999, placing one card on top of another (see Fig. 3.8).

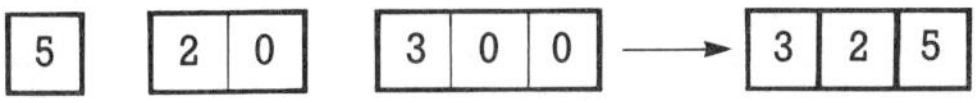

Fig. 3.8

Activities

1 Give the set of cards to a child in three piles – of units, tens and hundreds. Ask him or her to make up numbers called by the teacher, e.g. 'Make four hundred and twenty-six', etc.

2 Show a number on the blackboard, e.g. 738. Ask the class, 'How many tens have we here?', 'How many hundreds?', 'How many units?' Now show the number 738 made up from three place-value cards. Now split up the set to show $700 + 30 + 8$.

Large numeral cards, tens and units

This is a set of large cards (about 15 cm × 20 cm) on which are written, at the top, various numbers between 10 and 100. Cardboard ten-strips, or bundles of ten, and single units can be placed on the cards to the value of the number on the card. The ten-strips can be cut from stiff card and made *exactly* ten units long. These strips are preferably marked into ten equal sections of the same size as the units. Alternatively, bundles of ten sticks and single sticks can be used.

Activities

A child is given a card and tries to place the correct number of ten-strips (or bundles of ten) and units on the card. The teacher can easily check several of these completed cards while moving round the class. The backs of the cards can be used by the teacher to set out ten-strips and units for the pupil to record by writing the number down.

Place-value tins or pockets

These can be made easily from discarded tins or cardboard cartons. Note that since the tins or pockets are labelled H, T, U, it is not really necessary to put bundles of hundreds in the hundreds pocket and bundles of tens in the tens pocket. The tins or pockets can later be used in the same way as the spike abacus which follows.

A spike abacus

In an abacus, a counter represents either 1 or 10 or 100, depending on where it is placed. In the abacus in Figs. 3.9 and 3.10 the spikes are made from nails driven through a piece of wood ; the heads may need to be cut off and filed. Bottle tops with holes punched through the centre are used as counters. Each spike must hold *exactly nine counters* when full.

In Fig. 3.9 the three nails are each 10 cm long and the block of wood is about $3\frac{1}{2}$ cm thick. The spikes hold just nine bottle tops if these are placed as shown alternately 'down' and 'up'. Note that on each spike, an odd number shows with the top counter 'down' and an even number with the top counter 'up'. The number shown on the abacus is 419.

Fig. 3.9

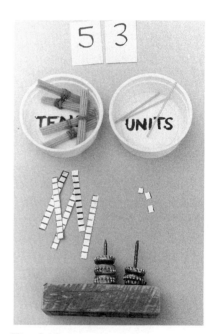

Fig. 3.10

Fig. 3.10 shows the same number, 53, represented in three different ways : tens (bundles) and units in tins, ten-strips and units, and on a spike abacus.

Representing numbers with marked cardboard strips and squares

Hundreds, tens and *units*   can be cut out of stiff card by marking out approximately one-centimetre squares. (The size of the squares is not important provided they are all the same.)

The number 243 is represented as shown in Fig. 3.11.

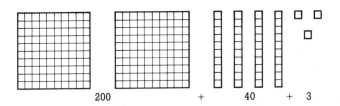

Fig. 3.11

3.3 ADDITION

3.31 Addition situations

Addition arises where two groups of objects or quantities are put together to form one larger group or amount.

Young children's first experiences with arithmetic are of crucial importance. Teachers must carefully plan ways of making the experiences enjoyable and meaningful. Pupils must see a need for addition and the other operations of arithmetic. Games often provide the motivation required.

1 Paint ten bottle tops with the numbers 0, 1, 2, . . . , 9. Put the tops in a paper bag. Two or more pupils take turns, each drawing out two tops at a time. The pupil whose total score is highest after each draw then takes a counter (a stick, or another bottle top). The game continues until one player has ten counters and is declared the winner.

2 Make a cardboard spinner as shown in Fig. 3.12. Pupils take turns to spin the top twice. The score is the total of the two numbers obtained. The winner after each round is the player who scores highest.

Fig. 3.12

3 A *class shop* provides a good means of teaching early addition. Use plastic bottles, tins and other discarded containers which have been cleaned. These articles must have their prices written clearly on them, using (small) whole numbers of units (dollars and cents). Flattened bottle tops, or circles cut from card, can be used as coins, labelled as 1 c and 5 c and, later, 10 c. Paper or card rectangles can be used as bank notes, where appropriate.

4 Once children are interested they can deal with more formal situations, such as:

> 'Here are three sticks. Here are another two sticks.
> How many sticks are there altogether?'

Note that there are two separate skills to teach:

(a)   Put out two piles of sticks. Ask the child to write the number of sticks underneath each pile. Then show how to put the two piles together and count the total number of sticks. Ask the child to write this number under the new pile.

(b)   Write out two numbers, or set out cards with the numbers written on them. Ask the child to put out the correct number of sticks under each number. Then proceed as in (a) above.

The objects used for counting can be sticks, stones, buttons, bottle tops, etc. In fact it is good to use a variety of objects, giving children wide experience of counting materials. Do not hurry children through this stage of counting: allow as much experience with physical objects as they need, to gain confidence with the early stages of arithmetic.

3.32   Language and vocabulary

It is very important to use the correct language of arithmetic with young children. This does not mean we should use long or complicated words, but we should use words accurately and consistently. Words should also be used only in meaningful situations. For example, 'I have six beans and I add three more beans. How many beans have I now?'

The following words are commonly used in the teaching of addition and care should be taken when teaching their meaning:

and	together make
altogether	add
more than	equals
is the same as	sum
plus	makes

3.33   Developing the addition algorithm

Begin by putting together counters such as bottle tops and counting the total number. This will enable pupils to find the total number in simple computations such as 4 + 3, 5 + 4, etc. Progress should then proceed as follows.

[Units] + [Units], totals more than 10

Vertical form could be introduced at this stage but without 'tens' and 'units' columns. A number track may be used along which the child can align the two given numbers of counters.

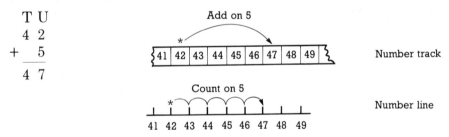

$$\begin{array}{r} 9 \\ + \ 5 \\ \hline 14 \end{array}$$

[Tens, Units] + [Units], no regrouping

Pupils can count on along the number track or number line until they reach the total. Counters may not be necessary at this stage. Tens and units columns should be introduced.

$$\begin{array}{r} \text{T U} \\ 4 \ 2 \\ + \ \ 5 \\ \hline 4 \ 7 \end{array}$$

Add on 5

| 41 | 42 | 43 | 44 | 45 | 46 | 47 | 48 | 49 | Number track

Count on 5

41 42 43 44 45 46 47 48 49   Number line

This is a suitable stage at which to teach the addition facts totalling less than 10 (see Section 3.34, p. 41).

[Tens, Units] + [Units], regrouping the units

$$\begin{array}{r} \text{T U} \\ 3 \ 8 \\ + \ \ 4 \\ \hline 4 \ 2 \end{array}$$

Place-value material such as bundles of tens and ones are suitable to use here (see Section 3.22, p. 34).

At this stage, children should be able to translate from horizontal form, e.g. $24 + 35$, to vertical form:

```
 T U
 2 4
+3 5
────

────
```

[Tens, Units] + [Tens, Units], without regrouping

```
 T U
 2 4
+3 5
────
 5 9
```

Place-value apparatus should be used if necessary (e.g. ten-strips and units).

To perform the addition algorithm efficiently by this stage pupils should have quick recall of addition facts with totals to 19.

[Tens, Units] + [Tens, Units], with regrouping

Use no learning aid other than an addition table if necessary. Units must be added before tens.

```
 2 8     2 8     2 8
+4 5    +4 5    +4 5
────    ────    ────
         3      7 3
────
   1
```

Note that pupils should now know that $8 + 5 = 13$. Alternatively, the 'carried' one can be placed in the tens column, either beside the 4 or beside the 2.

Addition of [Hundreds, Tens, Units]

Progress from examples without regrouping, such as

```
 H T U
 3 3 1
+1 2 5
──────
 4 5 6
```

to ones with regrouping on one column only,

```
 3 1 7          4 6 3
+2 6 4    or   +4 5 6
──────         ──────

──────         ──────
```

and then to examples with regrouping in two columns. Include some examples with two-digit numbers, e.g.

```
    4 3
+ 5 6 9
———————
```

This can be demonstrated with a 3-spike abacus (see Fig. 3.13).

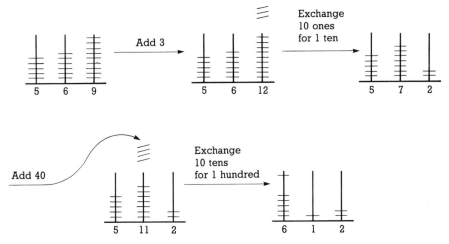

Fig. 3.13

After this stage, the labelling of the H, T and U columns can be dropped. Once pupils fully understand the algorithm for hundreds, tens and units, they should be able to apply it to larger numbers – thousands and above. There is no mathematical value in practising with larger and larger multi-digit numbers.

3.34 Teaching the addition facts

Demonstrating commutativity

All the basic addition facts can be written in two ways:

$$4 + 5 = 9 \quad \text{and} \quad 5 + 4 = 9$$

1 Make an addition square for the numbers up to ten (see Fig. 3.14). What do pupils notice? The numbers in diagonal strips are the same.

This shows that for each pair of numbers,

$$4 + 2 = 2 + 4, \quad 4 + 3 = 3 + 4, \quad \text{etc.}$$

This shows the *commutative* law for addition.

+	1	2	3	4	5	6	7	8	9	10
1										
2				6						
3				7						
4		6								
5		7								
6										
7										
8										
9										
10										

Fig. 3.14

2 Ask pupils to think of a story for, say, $3 + 5 = 8$.

I collected three mangoes, then a friend gave me five more. Then I had eight altogether. The next day I collected five mangoes and then a friend gave me three more; I had eight altogether.

Addition tables

These are simple to draw on the blackboard and pupils can then copy them into their books. The square is completed as shown in Fig. 3.15.

+	3	5	8
6			14	← 8 + 6
4		9	
7			15	← 8 + 7

Fig. 3.15

As pupils complete these squares, they will realise that it does not matter in which order the numbers are added (row to column, or column to row): the result is the same. These are excellent for giving pupils quick practice in addition facts between more formal work.

Flash cards

Flash cards should be made large enough for the pupils to see from the back of the classroom. They should be made as neatly and as professionally as possible. Addition of a pair of numbers should be on the front of the card and the answer should be written clearly on the reverse, e.g.

$$4 + 3 \qquad 7$$

Reverse of card

A game: Ten-up snap

Make about five sets of cards of the numbers 1 up to 9. Share the cards equally between three or four children. The children then place cards alternately on to a pile between them, with the numbers facing up. When two consecutive cards total ten, the first player to call 'Ten-up!' wins all the cards in the pile and adds them to the cards in his hand. The game continues until one child holds all the cards.

Splitting numbers

For this game with the whole class, the teacher calls out a number and then asks different pupils to give two smaller numbers which make up that number.

For example, the teacher chooses the number 8. The first pupil asked says, '2 and 6'. The next pupil asked says, '7 and 1', and so on.

There are five possible addition pairs of 8:

$$0 + 8, \quad 1 + 7, \quad 2 + 6, \quad 3 + 5, \quad 4 + 4$$

but many more pairs for larger numbers up to 20.

These can be demonstrated using number strips (see Fig. 3.16)

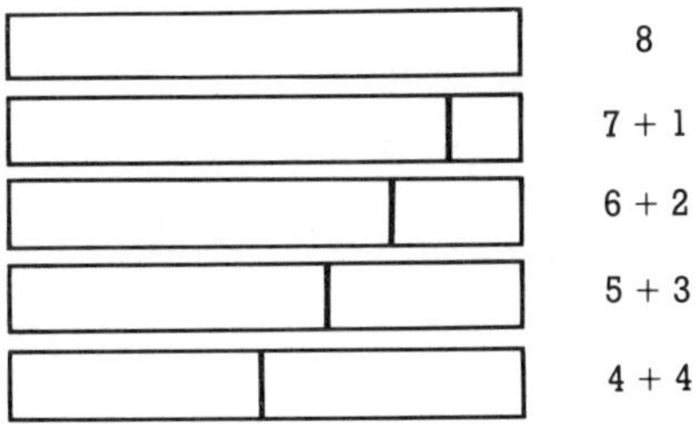

8

7 + 1

6 + 2

5 + 3

4 + 4

Fig. 3.16

Number pairs

The pairs of numbers with totals up to 10 are most important. Here are all the possible addition pairs totalling 10 or less (the commutative pairs are not included).

$$10 = 0 + 10 = 1 + 9 = 2 + 8 = 3 + 7 = 4 + 6 = 5 + 5$$

$$9 = 0 + 9 = 1 + 8 = 2 + 7 = 3 + 6 = 4 + 5$$

$$8 = 0 + 8 = 1 + 7 = 2 + 6 = 3 + 5 = 4 + 4$$

$$7 = 0 + 7 = 1 + 6 = 2 + 5 = 3 + 4$$

$$6 = 0 + 6 = 1 + 5 = 2 + 4 = 3 + 3$$

$$5 = 0 + 5 = 1 + 4 = 2 + 3$$

$$4 = 0 + 4 = 1 + 3 = 2 + 2$$

$$3 = 0 + 3 = 1 + 2$$

$$2 = 0 + 2 = 1 + 1$$

Write these pairs on a sheet of paper, stick it to a card sheet and cut up into cards for pupils to work with. Pupils can keep their cards in a matchbox and discard each written fact as it is learnt. The answers can be written on the back of each card if required.

Stages in teaching the addition facts

1 Adding on 1 – the full staircase (see Fig. 3.17a)

$$\ldots, \quad 4 + 1 = 5, \quad 5 + 1 = 6, \quad \ldots$$

2 Adding on 2 – the odd and even staircases (see Fig. 3.17b)

$$1 + 2 = 3, \quad 3 + 2 = 5, \quad 5 + 2 = 7, \quad 7 + 2 = 9$$
$$2 + 2 = 4, \quad 4 + 2 = 6, \quad 6 + 2 = 8, \quad 8 + 2 = 10$$

3 Knowledge of doubles

$$1 + 1 = 2, \quad 2 + 2 = 4, \quad 3 + 3 = 6, \quad \ldots$$

4 Relating near-doubles to doubles

$$7 + 8 = (7 + 7) + 1, \quad 9 + 8 = (8 + 8) + 1$$

5 Equal bonds (see *Splitting numbers*, p. 43)

$$8 + 1 = 7 + 2 = 6 + 3$$

6 Adding on 10

$$1 + 10 = 11, \quad 2 + 10 = 12, \quad 3 + 10 = 13, \quad \ldots$$

7 Zero facts (0 is the *identity element* for addition)

$$8 + 0 = 8, \quad 0 + 10 = 10$$

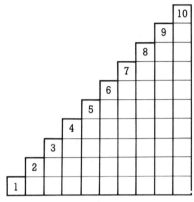 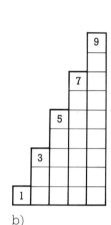 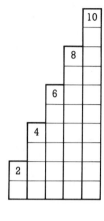

Fig. 3.17   a)   b)

3.4 SUBTRACTION

3.41 Subtraction situations

Subtraction occurs in two distinct everyday contexts, which we may call *take away* and *comparison*. Here are some examples.

Take away

'I had seven mangoes and then I lost three of them. Now I have only four.'

From the set of seven mangoes we take away three, leaving four.

$$7 - 3 = 4$$

Comparison

'I have seven mangoes and Peter has three mangoes. How many more mangoes do I have than Peter?'

Comparing seven with three, I find that I have four mangoes more than Peter.

$$7 - 3 = 4$$

The difference between 7 and 3 is 4.

Note that in the take-away situation, we start with only seven mangoes, whilst in the comparison situation we have 10 mangoes altogether.

Formal subtraction situations

Subtraction can also be shown at a later stage in more formal mathematical contexts which we may refer to as *missing number*, *inverse addition* and *counting back*.

These are illustrated by the following examples.

Missing number

$$4 + ? = 10$$
$$? + 6 = 9$$

Here, the number missing in the addition sentence can be found by subtracting. This can be seen as a *difference* situation; we have to find the *difference between* 4 and 10 or between 6 and 9, etc.

Inverse addition

Every addition fact can be rewritten as two subtraction facts:

$5 + 3 = 8$ implies that $8 - 3 = 5$ and $8 - 5 = 3$
$5 + 8 = 13$ implies that $13 - 5 = 8$ and $13 - 8 = 5$

Counting back

$9 - 3$ can be found by counting back 3 from 9:

$$9 \rightarrow 8 \rightarrow 7 \rightarrow 6 \quad \text{so,} \quad 9 - 3 = 6$$

Similarly,

$17 - 5: \quad 17 \rightarrow 16 \rightarrow 15 \rightarrow 14 \rightarrow 13 \rightarrow 12, \quad \text{so} \quad 17 - 5 = 12$

3.42 Language and vocabulary

We use subtraction in many different contexts. Take care to use the correct words for each situation. Words and phrases include:

take away	fewer than	more than
greater than	how many are left?	difference between
less than	how many more/less?	minus
subtract		

3.43 Introducing subtraction

Use physical objects to demonstrate the first subtraction situations to a child.

'You have five beans. I am going to take two of them away from you', How many beans do you have now? Count them: one, two, three. Now you have three.'

'Five take away two leaves three. Write this.' $(5 - 2 = 3)$
We can say, 'Five *minus* two *equals* three'.

Later, give pupils examples such as the above and ask them to find the
answers using a small collection of beans or other counting objects. For
example, 'What is $8 - 3$?'

This question asks, 'How many are left when we have eight beans and
three of them are taken away?' The child picks up eight beans, puts
three of them away on one side, counts those which are left and records
the result: $8 - 3 = 5$.

Use various materials and situations to demonstrate the basic *take
away* principle and vary the language slightly from time to time to create
a full understanding. For example,

'There are six cows in a field but four of them wander away. How many
cows are left?'
'Eight birds are sitting on a wire. Then three of them fly away. How
many of them remain on the wire?'
'I buy five bottles of Coke but on the way home I drop two of them.
How many bottles do I still have?'

Later, introduce the *comparison* situation. For example,

'I have four beans, and you have nine beans. You have more beans
than me. How many more?'

Demonstrate this by laying out the beans in two rows. Show the *one-to-
one correspondence* between the rows as far as it goes. The unmatched
beans in the greater row show us that the answer to the question is five
beans:

$$9 - 4 = 5$$

3.44   Developing the subtraction algorithm

Our aim in teaching subtraction is that children should be able to carry
out subtraction of multi-digit numbers confidently and accurately,
using one or other of the standard algorithms. However, at every stage of
development, pupils may need to use simple learning aids – counters
and other apparatus described earlier. They should not be discouraged
from doing so, but once they understand the processes they are carrying
out, most pupils will want to work without the 'crutches' they are using.

The *decomposition* method is widely accepted today as the easiest for
children to understand and is the method used here in the stages of
development which follow. Details of two other methods which have
been popular at different times are given at the end of this section.

[Units] − [Units]

Children can use counters such as beans or count back along the number track, e.g.

$$7 - 2, \quad 9 - 5, \quad 6 - 3$$

[Tens, Units] − [Units]

Children can count back along the number track or use their knowledge of subtraction facts from 0 to 20. Note the third example here extends the 'counting back' into the previous decade (0–9):

$$17 - 3, \quad 19 - 8, \quad 15 - 7$$

At a later stage, pupils will see $15 - 7$ as $15 - (5 + 2)$ i.e. count back 5 to 10, and then 2 more.

It can also be seen as $10 + 5 - 7 = (10 - 7) + 5$, i.e. 7 is 3 less than 10, plus another 5 to make 8; this is really a *complementary addition* (see Section 3.47, p. 53).

This is a suitable point at which to introduce the *subtraction facts* (Section 3.45, p. 50).

This stage can be extended to numbers up to 100, e.g.

$$67 - 3, \quad 85 - 7$$

Pupils may use a number line, or a 1–100 number square.

Vertical layout of [Tens, Units], no regrouping (decomposition)

[Tens, Units] − [Units]

$$\begin{array}{r} 27 \\ - \ 3 \\ \hline 24 \end{array}$$ Illustrate with place-value material.

[Tens, Units] − [Tens, Units]

$$\begin{array}{r} 85 \\ - 43 \\ \hline 42 \end{array}$$ Blackboard layout, for pupils to copy: $$\begin{array}{r} 85 \rightarrow 80 + 5 \\ - 43 \rightarrow 40 + 3 \\ \hline \leftarrow 40 + 2 \end{array}$$

Subtraction of [Tens, Units] with regrouping

[Tens, Units] – [Units]
Use place-value material.

$$\begin{array}{r} 32 \\ -\ 8 \\ \hline 24 \end{array}$$

Ten-bundles of sticks can be unbundled to give extra units. (Ten-strips can be exchanged for ten units.) Now take the 8 away from the 12 separate sticks to leave four sticks and two tens.

[Tens, Units] – [Tens, Units]

$$\begin{array}{r} 64 \\ -\ 19 \\ \hline 45 \end{array}$$ Use place value material for this in the same way.

We cannot subtract 9 from 4, so need to split or *decompose* a ten into units, giving 50 and 14 units: $14 - 9 = 5$. This reasoning can be set out in the following blackboard layout:

$$\begin{array}{l} 64 \rightarrow 60 + 4 \rightarrow 50 + 14 \\ -\,19 \rightarrow 10 + 9 \rightarrow 10 +\ \ 9 \\ \hline 45 \leftarrow \qquad\qquad 40 +\ \ 5 \end{array}$$

This can later be contracted
to

$$\begin{array}{r} ^5\!6^1\!4 \\ -\ 1\ 9 \\ \hline 4\ 5 \end{array}$$

and eventually pupils may omit the / and the 'crutch' digits.

Subtraction of [Hundreds, Tens, Units]
The decomposition algorithm can gradually be extended to cope with subtraction of any two 3-digit numbers:

No regrouping

$$\begin{array}{r} 639 \\ -\,418 \\ \hline \end{array}$$

Regrouping in one place

$$\begin{array}{r} 728 \\ -\,543 \\ \hline \end{array} \quad \text{or} \quad \begin{array}{r} 540 \\ -\,217 \\ \hline \end{array}$$

Regrouping in two places

a) $\begin{array}{r} 805 \\ -\,329 \\ \hline \end{array}$ b) $\begin{array}{r} 500 \\ -\,126 \\ \hline \end{array}$

Note the special problem of zeros in the top line.

a) $805 \rightarrow 700 + 100 + 5 \rightarrow 700 + 90 + 15$ or ${}^{7}\!\cancel{8}{}^{9}\!\cancel{0}{}^{1}5$

    $-\,329 \rightarrow 300 + 20 + 9 \rightarrow 300 + 20 + 9$ $-\,3\ 2\ 9$

    $476 \leftarrow$ $400 + 70 + 6$ $4\ 7\ 6$

b) ${}^{4}\!\cancel{5}{}^{10}\!\cancel{0}{}^{\overset{9}{10}1}0$

                     $-\ 1\ \ 2\ 6$

                      $3\ \ 7\ 4$

Extension to numbers over 1000

There are no new techniques to be taught. Children who can handle 3-digit numbers confidently should be able to work with larger ones. For all practical purposes, however, computation with 4-digit numbers is quite sufficient.

3.45   Teaching the subtraction facts

There are fifty-five subtraction facts involving numbers up to ten which children need to recall quickly. They can be learnt by pupils either by rote (repetition) or in a game or puzzle situation.

These facts or number bonds are:

$9-9$	$9-8$	$9-7$	$9-6$	$9-5$	$9-4$	$9-3$	$9-2$	$9-1$	$9-0$
	$8-8$	$8-7$	$8-6$	$8-5$	$8-4$	$8-3$	$8-2$	$8-1$	$8-0$
		$7-7$	$7-6$	$7-5$	$7-4$	$7-3$	$7-2$	$7-1$	$7-0$
			$6-6$	$6-5$	$6-4$	$6-3$	$6-2$	$6-1$	$6-0$
				$5-5$	$5-4$	$5-3$	$5-2$	$5-1$	$5-0$
					$4-4$	$4-3$	$4-2$	$4-1$	$4-0$
						$3-3$	$3-2$	$3-1$	$3-0$
							$2-2$	$2-1$	$2-0$
								$1-1$	$1-0$
									$0-0$

However, to carry out more difficult subtraction confidently later, using one of the standard algorithms, children need quick recall of all the facts up to $18 - 9$.

This provides all the subtraction facts needed when carrying out regrouping. (The answers are all single-digit numbers.)

Subtraction tables

These are similar to addition tables (see Section 3.34, p. 41) but with the rule that the numbers in the vertical column should be subtracted from the numbers in the top row.

$-$	7	9	11	
4			7	$\leftarrow 11-4$
6		3		
3			8	$\leftarrow 11-3$

Fig. 3.18

Flash cards

Flash cards similar to those described on p. 43 can be used.

$10 - 4$		6

Reverse of card

Stages in teaching subtraction facts

1 Begin by asking pupils to count backwards.

2 Later, ask them to count back in tens.

3 Pay particular attention to subtractions resulting in zero, since this is a very common source of error with pupils (see next section).

3.46 Common errors in subtraction

1 Subtracting the larger digit from the smaller, irrespective of position:

$$\begin{array}{r} 4\ 5 \\ -\ \overset{1}{2}\ 8 \\ \hline 2\ 3 \end{array}$$

Remedy Ask the pupil to make up the two numbers with sticks and ten-bundles. 'Take away' by physically regrouping.

2 Errors with exchange notation:

$$
\begin{array}{r}
4\ {}^{1}5 \\
-\,\not{2}^{1}\ 8 \\
\hline
3\ 7
\end{array}
$$

Remedy Show the meaning of the correct notation – see blackboard demonstration on p. 49.

3 Errors of alignment:

$$
\begin{array}{r}
3\ 7\ 6 \\
-\,2\ 5 \\
\hline
1\ 2\ 6
\end{array}
\qquad
\begin{array}{r}
2\ 1\ 4 \\
1\ 8 \\
\hline
1\ 6
\end{array}
$$

Remedy Ensure that the pupil uses squared paper and sets columns out correctly; if necessary, provide paper with larger squares.

Encourage children to check any subtraction by 'adding upwards' in vertical layout, the two lower lines should add together to give the top line. The 'crutch' figure in the decomposition then becomes the 'carry' figure in the addition:

$$
\begin{array}{r}
6\ {}^{'}5 \\
-\,2\ 8 \\
\hline
3\ 7
\end{array}
\qquad
\begin{array}{r}
3\ 7 \\
+\,2\ 8 \\
\hline
6\ {}^{'}5
\end{array}
$$

3.47 Other subtraction algorithms

Equal additions

This method is still widely used, especially among people who have good number ability. It is possibly a more efficient and quicker method than decomposition, but initially it is harder for children to understand. The principle involved is that the *difference between* two numbers remains the same when *both are increased* by the same amount. A useful analogy is to have two children of different height come to the front of the class and ask, 'How much taller is Jane than Peter?' Now have both children stand on a bench; ask again, 'How much taller...? Has the amount changed?'

The following examples illustrate the method:

$$\begin{array}{r} 64 \\ -\,19 \\ \hline \end{array} \quad \text{Using 'crutch' digits:} \quad \begin{array}{r} 6\,{}^{1}4 \\ -\,{}^{2}\not{1}\,9 \\ \hline 4\;5 \end{array}$$

We cannot subtract 9 from 4, so add 10 units to the top number. We must also add 10 (1 ten) to the lower number. The expanded layout on the left can be used.

$$\begin{array}{rcccl} 64 & \rightarrow & 60+4 & \rightarrow & 60+14 \\ -\,19 & \rightarrow & 10+9 & \rightarrow & 20+\;\,9 \\ \hline 45 & \leftarrow & & & 40+\;\,5 \end{array}$$

$$\begin{array}{r} 3000 \\ -\,1724 \\ \hline 1276 \end{array}$$

The separate subtractions here are $10-4$, $10-3$, $10-8$, $3-2$.
With decomposition they would be $10-4$, $9-2$, $9-7$, $2-1$.

The same principle could be used in different ways to speed up computation, especially when done mentally:

$$324-195 = 329-200 = 129$$

Complementary addition

This method is, in fact, used very widely in giving change (money) in shops. It is also the easiest method to use with units of time. We *add on* to the smaller number or quantity until we reach the larger one.

To take a simple example, $36-17$ can be calculated as

'17 and **3** make 20, and another **16** make 36, so $36-17$ is 19'.

One advantage of this method is that it does not need the 'extended' subtraction facts, but only those up to ten. (see Section 3.45, p. 50).

There are various ways of 'thinking through' the algorithm: the one suggested in the following example has the merit of being mathematically logical.

$$\begin{array}{r} 8\;05 \\ -\;{}^{1}4\,{}^{1}29 \\ \hline 3\;76 \end{array}$$

'9 needs 1 to make it 10; $1+5$ is 6. (29 has been built up to 30.) 3 needs 7 to make it 10. (430 has been built up to 500.) $8-5$ is 3.'

The 'crutch' digits remind us that we have 'built up' in those places. A number line can also be used to explain the method (see Fig. 3.19).

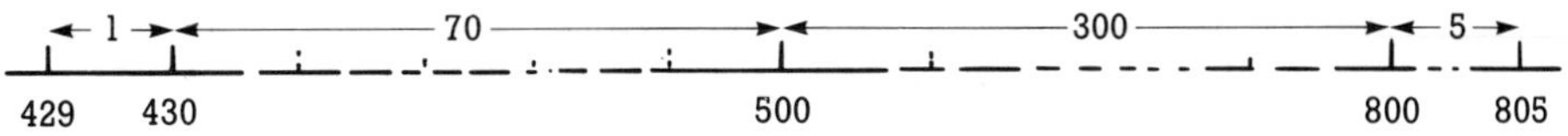

Fig. 3.19

Whatever method children are taught, the language they use should make sense and correspond with what they are actually doing. Note that, in *none* of the methods discussed is there 'borrowing' or 'paying back'.

3.5 MULTIPLICATION

3.51 Language of multiplication

When we are counting many equal groups of objects, a knowledge of multiplication saves us time:

If we have five groups of four beans, the total number of beans is $4 + 4 + 4 + 4 + 4$, but we can write this more concisely as 5×4, that is '5 *lots of* 4', or '5 4's', or '5 *times* 4'. It is usually thought to be more natural to interpret 5×4 as '5 lots of 4' rather than '4 lots of 5' or '5 *multiplied* by 4'.

Teachers can introduce children to multiplication by providing examples of equal groups. For example,

'There are four children here; each child has two hands. How many hands is that altogether?'

'Here are six matchboxes; each box contains three beans. How many beans is that altogether?'

'A book costs four dollars; how much do we need for three books?'

3.52 Introducing the special properties of multiplication

Children can be led to the multiplication results by:

1 Grouping objects or counters in equal groups

2 Taking equal steps along a number track or line

3 Marking equal steps on a 100 number square.

1 Children can arrange counters in equal groups and record their findings. For example, for groups of 3 counters:

One group of 3 is 3 $1 \times 2 = 3$
Two groups of 3 are 6 $2 \times 3 = 6$
Three groups of 3 are 9 $3 \times 3 = 9$

2 a) Using a number track, and number strips of a certain length, children can record their results.

1	2	3	4	5	6	7	8	9	10	11	12	13

e.g.   One 4 is 4 $1 \times 4 = 4$
                       Two 4s are 8 $2 \times 4 = 8$
                       Three 4s are 12 $3 \times 4 = 12$

b) Using a number line, mark off equal steps with arrows and record the results as above.

3 Children can mark equal steps on a 100 number square and record their observations.

3.53 Commutative property of multiplication

By comparing their results for, say, three lots of four and four lots of three, children come to understand that, for any pair of factors, the order in which they are written does not matter. This is the commutative law which holds for multiplication just as it does for addition (see Section 3.34, p. 41).

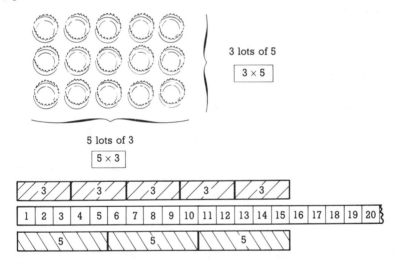

Fig. 3.20

When counters are arranged in a rectangular array, they can be counted in rows or in columns. In Fig. 3.20 there are five columns each containing three bottle tops, and three rows each containing five bottle tops. Using a number track or line, we can see that $3 \times 5 = 5 \times 3$.

3.54 Multiplying by zero and by one

Set out five matchboxes, each containing three beans. The number of beans altogether is $3 + 3 + 3 + 3 + 3$ or 5×3. Now remove all the beans, each box contains 0 beans. The total number is therefore $0 + 0 + 0 + 0 + 0$ or 5×0, but, clearly, this is 0. In this way, children can understand that any number 'times 0' gives 0.

Even if they have grasped the commutative law, it is harder to understand that '0 times' any number is also 0. This can be shown by starting with several equal groups and then taking them away, one group at a time.

Start with four matchboxes, each containing three beans:

$4 \times 3 = 12$
Now remove one box of beans $3 \times 3 = 9$
Now remove another box $2 \times 3 = 6$
Remove another box $1 \times 3 = 3$
Now remove the last box; there are no boxes, so $0 \times 3 = 0$.

Zero is the main cause of mistakes in multiplication. Unless this special property of 0 is known, and practised, pupils will make errors such as $0 \times 5 = 5$, or even $0 \times 5 = 1$! In any revision test or quiz, the teacher should include one or two products containing zero.

The special role of 1

1 is sometimes called the *identity element* for multiplication. All the separate multiplication tables start with a product of 1.

$$4 \times 1 = 4 \quad \text{or} \quad 1 \times 8 = 8$$

When 1 is a factor in a product, the other factor is unchanged by the multiplication.

3.55   Teaching the multiplication algorithm

The aim is for children to carry out long multiplication confidently and accurately. In practice, they will rarely, if ever, need to multiply together numbers which together contain more than six digits, i.e. thousands and tens, or hundreds and hundreds. If they can perform such multiplications efficiently, then they have mastered the algorithm, and there is no point in giving practice with still larger numbers.

The development of multiplication falls naturally into several stages:

Quick recall of the multiplication facts

Teachers should give the class regular oral practice to reinforce knowledge of the tables.

[Tens, Units] × [Units] no regrouping

Use place-value material, setting out tens and units in columns.

```
 32
×  3
―――
 96
```

96 sticks

[Tens, Units] × [Units] with regrouping

Products greater than 100

For example

```
 32
×   4
―――
128
```

Four 2s are 8. Four 3s are 12. There are 12 tens : 10 tens are a hundred, so we need a hundreds column.

Product contains more than 10 units

The units must be regrouped, 'carrying' into the tens column.

For example

```
 23
×  4
―――
 92
```

Fig. 3.21 shows the process of regrouping, using sticks for units and ten-bundles.

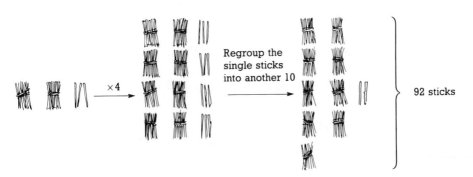

Fig. 3.21

Multiplication by 10

Set out 2 ten-strips and 3 units, and repeat 10 times. Regroup the material as shown in Fig. 3.22. Notice that we have 2 hundred-squares and 3 ten-strips. After several examples of this kind, pupils can accept the rule that multiplying by 10 *moves each digit one place to the left*.

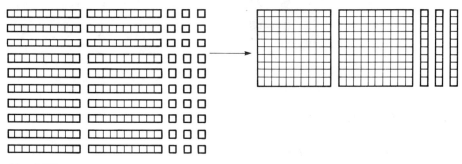

Fig. 3.22

Multiples of 10, 20, 30, ...

Using place-value material children discover that, for example, $2 \times 30 = 60$. The commutative law tells us that $30 \times 2 = 60$, so $30 \times 2 = 10 \times (3 \times 2)$.

When multiplying 3 or more factors, they can be grouped in any way: $(10 \times 3) \times 2 = 10 \times (3 \times 2)$. This is the *associative* property of '×', although the term should not be used with pupils.

Following the previous stage, this means that, to multiply by 30, we multiply by 3 and then by 10, moving the digits one place to the left.

The distributive law

We say that '×' *is distributive over* '+', although this term should not be taught to pupils.

The stages on p. 57 show that, for example, $4 \times 32 = (4 \times 30) + (4 \times 2)$. This principle is important in developing the algorithm. It can be introduced to pupils much earlier: for example, Fig. 3.23 shows that

$$2 \times 3 \ + \ 4 \times 3 \ = \ 6 \times 3$$

```
       **        ****      ******

       **   +  ****    =   ******

       **        ****      ******
```

Fig. 3.23

Extending the algorithm

All the previous stages can be brought together for long multiplication. To start with, pupils can label the *partial products* as shown below:

```
    32                208                  341
  × 16              ×  35                ×  173
  ─────             ──────               ──────
   320  (10 × 32)    6240  (30 × 208)     34100  (100 × 341)
   192  ( 6 × 32)    1040  ( 5 × 208)     23870  ( 70 × 341)
  ─────             ──────                1023  (  3 × 341)
   512  (16 × 32)    7280  (35 × 208)    ──────
                                         58993  (173 × 341)
```

3.56 Teaching the multiplication facts

Number patterns

Using a 100 number square, place counters at equal intervals (or mark them with circles).

Children can investigate the various patterns made for different steps.

Building up multiplication tables

To reinforce the commutative property, children should build up each table in two ways. Fig. 3.24 shows, on the left, the *table of 3s* : and on the right the *3 times table*.

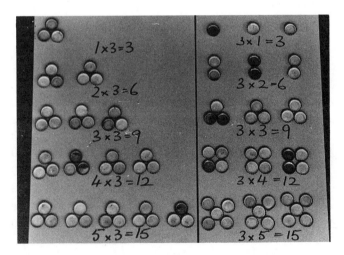

Fig. 3.24

Teachers can build up the tables in different orders. Remember, however, that the easiest table to memorise is the *table of tens*; if children have a secure understanding of place-value, then they know that

$$1 \times 10 = 10$$

$$2 \times 10 = 20$$

$$3 \times 10 = 30$$

. . .

The *table of twos* is the sequence of *even numbers*, and this is therefore one of the earliest for pupils to memorise.

The *table of fives* has a pattern which is easy to remember:

$$5 \quad 10 \quad 15 \quad 20 \quad 25 \quad 30 \quad . . .$$

Children should note that 5 is half of 10, so the steps in the table carry them halfway along the next ten. Note also that *doubling* 5 gives 10. Other tables can be formed by doubling, e.g.

$$2 \times \text{table} \to 4 \times \text{table} \to 8 \times \text{table, and } 3 \times \text{table} \to 6 \times \text{table.}$$

In fact, *doubling* and *halving* are important skills. The hardest tables are probably those for seven and eight.

The *table of nines* also has a pattern which children should explore:

$$9 \quad 18 \quad 27 \quad 36 \quad 45 \quad 54 \quad 63 \quad 72 \quad 81 \quad 90$$

The units digit decreases as the tens digit increases: this is because adding on 9 is the same as adding 10 and subtracting 1. The sum of the digits is 9 in each case.

All the separate multiplication tables can be brought together in a square:

×	1	2	3	4	5	6	7	8	9	10
1	1	2	3	4	5	6	7	8	9	10
2	2	4	6	8	10	12	14	16	18	20
3	3	6	9	12	15	18	21	24	27	30
4	4	8	12	16	20	24	28	32	36	40
5	5	10	15	20	25	30	35	40	45	50
6	6	12	18	24	30	36	42	48	54	60
7	7	14	21	28	35	42	49	56	63	70
8	8	16	24	32	40	48	56	64	72	80
9	9	18	27	36	45	54	63	72	81	90
10	10	20	30	40	50	60	70	80	90	100

Note that, because of the commutative property, nearly half of the facts in this square table are included twice. The exceptions are the *square* numbers down the diagonal:

$$1 \quad 4 \quad 9 \quad 16 \quad \ldots$$

3.6 DIVISION

3.61 Division situations

There are two kinds of division problem which occur in everyday situations. These different aspects of division are known as *repeated subtraction* and *sharing*. However, both kinds of problem are solved formally by the same computation, namely $12 \div 4$.

Repeated subtraction

Consider the problem, 'I have 12 cards. To how many children can I give four cards each?'

Subtracting four cards at a time from a pack of 12, we find that we can do this three times. The answer is therefore 'Three children'.

Sharing

Consider the problem, 'Four children share 12 cards equally between them. How many cards does each child receive?'

Dealing the cards into four piles, we continue until no cards are left, and find that there are three in each pile. The answer is 'Three cards each'.

3.62 Language of division

Much confusion can arise through traditional use of the language of division. The following words and phrases occur in division situations associated with the symbols $12 \div 3$:

group 12 in 3s	divide 12 between 3
share 12 (equally) between 3	divide 3 into 12
divide 12 by 3	3 goes into 12
how many times does 3 go into 12?	

Therefore, great care must be taken by the teacher when explaining examples of division to children.

In $28 \div 7 = 4$, 28 is the *dividend*, 7 the *divisor* and 4 the *quotient*. (In this example there is no *remainder*.)

It is not necessary to teach these words to young children, except for *remainder* which arises naturally (see Section 3.64, p. 62).

3.63   Introducing the special properties of division

Division is best introduced through its *sharing* aspect, which is a natural situation for children. For example,

'Here are eight nuts. I want you to share them with your friend. How many each will you get?'

We can record it like this, $8 \div 2 = 4$. We say, 'Eight nuts shared between two children is four nuts each'. The teacher should use real objects – bottle tops, beans, etc. – and have two children to actually share them out on their desks. Then progress to more objects shared between more children. At this stage, make sure that there are no remainders.

Later, children should be given simple problems to solve using a number track or line, or number strips, e.g.

a) How many steps of three units are required to reach zero, starting from 12?

b) To reach 12 in three steps, how long must each step be?

Notice that (b) requires 'trial and error', or knowledge of multiplication tables, in finding the right length for each of the three steps: it is a sharing problem, i.e. $3 \times ? = 12$, whereas (a) is repeated subtraction.

The results of problems such as these can be recorded. The teacher needs to relate them to the multiplication facts which children should already know:

$$12 = 3 \times 4, \quad \text{so} \quad 12 \div 3 = 4, \quad \text{and} \quad 12 \div 4 = 3$$

3.64   Remainders

Give children further repeated subtraction and sharing problems using physical materials, but now leaving remainders, e.g.

'I have 13 beans. To how many children can I give five beans each?'

The answer is 'Two *children*, and three *beans* remain'. This is a repeated subtraction problem.

'I have 14 beans, and share them equally between four children. How many beans does each child receive, and how many are left over?'

The answer is 'Each child receives three beans, and two beans are left.' This is a sharing problem.

We can show remainders on a number line, e.g.

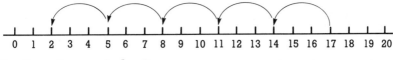

$17 \div 3 = 5$, remainder 2.

In this example, steps of 3 have been counted back from 17, but they could equally well be counted forward from 0, as in multiplication.

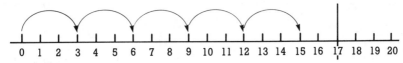

Five steps of three reach 15. This is two less than 17.

3.65 Teaching the division facts

Just as subtraction is the *inverse* of addition, so division is the *inverse* of multiplication. Every multiplication sentence can be rewritten in two ways as division:

$$3 \times 6 = 18 \quad \text{gives} \quad 18 \div 3 = 6 \quad \text{and} \quad 18 \div 6 = 3$$

Therefore, when a child is learning multiplication facts, he or she is also learning division facts. So to answer the question, 'What is 56 divided by seven?' a pupil should ask, 'Seven multiplied by what is 56?' or, 'What multiplies seven to make 56?'

3.66 Developing the division algorithm

[Tens, Units] ÷ [Units] without regrouping or remainders

Use place value material to illustrate sharing, as in Fig. 3.25.

$39 \div 3$

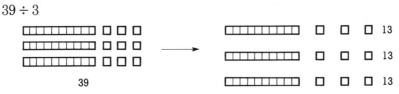

Fig. 3.25

We say, 'Three tens shared between three children is one ten each. Nine ones shared between three children is three ones each'.

This is recorded as $3\overline{)39}^{\,13}$

[Tens, Units] ÷ [Units] with regrouping, no remainders

42 ÷ 3 (see Fig. 3.26)

```
  TU
  1 4
3 | 4 2
  3
  ---
  1 2
```

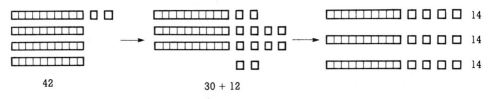

Fig. 3.26

Division with remainder

53 ÷ 4 (see Fig. 3.27)

```
   TU
   1 3
4 | 5 3
   4
   ---
   1 3
   1 2
   ---
   1
```

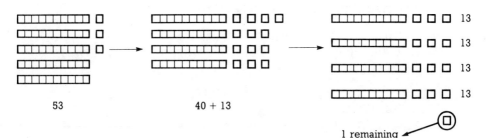

Fig. 3.27

When the divisor is a small number such as 2, 3, 4 or 5, the sharing process can be shown clearly using place value material. However, for larger divisors, the amount of material required makes its use cumbersome. The full algorithm may in any case be seen more easily as a *counting back* (repeated subtraction) situation.

53 ÷ 4 (alternative working)
How many 4s in 5? Answer, 1.
Set 1 down in tens column. 1 ten left over. The ten and 3 make 13.
How many 4s in 13? Answer, 3.
Set 3 down in units column.

It is important to teach division facts involving 10 (and later 100, etc.)
separately.

Division of 20, 30, 40 ...

The multiplication facts include the 10 times table and table of 10s.
Children who know, for example, that $3 \times 10 = 30$ should be able to
rewrite this as

$$30 \div 3 = 10, \quad 30 \div 10 = 3$$

Hence $$60 \div 3 = 20, \quad 80 \div 2 = 40, \quad \text{etc.}$$

Extend this to division of 200, 300, ... , e.g.

$$500 \div 5, \quad 600 \div 3, \quad \text{etc.}$$

Short division of [Hundred, Tens, Units] by [Units]

Introduce this by setting the division out in the traditional long division
form, with the quotient above the dividend:

```
    H T U
    1 4 5
3 | 4 3 5
    3
   ─────
    1 3
    1 2
   ─────
      1 5
      1 5
     ─────
      0 0
```

This can later be contracted to $3 | 4^1 3^1 5$ with $1\,4\,5$ above.

Long division of [Hundreds, Tens, Units] by [Tens, Units]

Divisors need not exceed 20, at least to start with. First write out the
stations of the divisor, i.e. a list of multiples. For example, when dividing
by 17:

1	2	3	4	5	6	7	8	9
17	34	51	68	85	102	119	136	153

Pupils should then carry out several divisions by 17, using this same list of multiples.

$$
\begin{array}{r}
38 \\
17\overline{\smash{\big)}\,653} \\
51 \\
\hline
143 \\
136 \\
\hline
7
\end{array}
$$

65 is more than 51, less than 68. 143 is more than 136, less than 153.

$653 \div 17 = 38$, remainder 7.
Note that $653 = (17 \times 38) + 7$.

3.7 ALGEBRA

In basic work with number operations we ask pupils to find the missing numbers in examples such as

$$\square + 6 = 10 \quad \text{or} \quad ? + 6 = 10$$

$$5 - \square = 2 \quad \text{or} \quad 5 - ? = 2$$

It is a natural step from these to write some other symbol, rather than an empty box or a question mark, to stand for the missing number:

$$a + 6 = 10$$

What does a stand for?

In this way we introduce the idea of a letter representing a number. A letter should always stand for a number, not an object, a person, a measurement or a sum of money. For example, if we say, 'There are n children in this classroom', n is not a child : it is the number of children. 'There are m mangoes in this basket' : m is the number of mangoes, not a mango! If a journey takes t hours, then t is the number of hours, and so on.

FOR THE TEACHER TO MAKE

A missing number box

Collect about 20 bottle tops and make a hole in the centre of each. Make a small hole in the centre of the base of a used cylindrical tin which has had the lid removed (a 1 kg margarine tin, or a 250 g coffee tin would be suitable). Thread a length of string through the base of the tin and also through 10 (or more) of the bottle tops. Knot the end outside the base so that it will not pull through the hole.

Use the apparatus as shown in Fig. 3.28. First let the class see how many tops are on the string. Then hide some of them inside the tin: the n on the tin represents the number of counters hidden. Write the equation for n on the blackboard.

$$n + 4 = 10$$

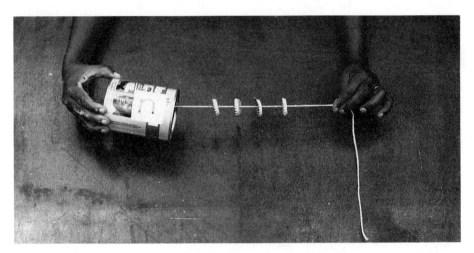

Fig. 3.28

3.71 Equations

In a mathematical sentence or equation, letters can have only certain values if the sentence is to be true. For example,

$$a + 6 = 10$$

is true only if a has the value 4, and we say that $a = 4$ is the solution of the equation.

Missing number sentences such as those in the previous section are the simplest kind of equation that we can devise. Give children practice in solving such equations orally, or by writing the solutions. Be sure to include equations using all four basic operations. Discuss them informally with the class, e.g.

'If $n - 3 = 7$, then n must be larger than 3, because subtracting 3 leaves 7. So n must be 3 more than 7, that is, 10.'

All of the following can be solved immediately by inspection. Note, however, that those in the right-hand column would normally at a later stage be written algebraically in a different form, without $\times$ and $\div$ signs.

$$a + 4 = 10 \qquad\qquad 3 \times e = 12$$
$$5 + b = 12 \qquad\qquad f \times 5 = 15$$
$$c - 6 = 7 \qquad\qquad g \div 2 = 8$$
$$9 - d = 2 \qquad\qquad 10 \div h = 5$$

3.72 Equations with two operations

An appropriate aim for top primary classes might be the solution of equations such as

$$3x - 5 = 7$$
$$2(n + 3) = 26$$

In these equations, two number operations are involved on the left of the equals sign.

The teacher can introduce these by a class game called 'Think of a number'. This develops pupils' ideas of operations and the order in which they are used. For example:

Teacher says, 'Think of a number;

add 3 to it;

now double what you have;

tell me what you have now.'

The pupil tells the teacher that this number is 26 and the teacher replies that the original number was 10.

The steps can be likened to wrapping up a parcel ('First wrap it in paper, then tie string round it'), which the teacher then has to unwrap ('First untie the string, then unwrap the paper').

$$n \xrightarrow{\text{Add 3}} n + 3 \xrightarrow{\text{Multiply by 2}} 2(n+3) \qquad (= 26)$$

We work backwards from 26 'unwrapping' the parcel, from right to left, 'reversing' or inverting the operations as we go:

$$10 \xleftarrow{\text{Subtract 3}} 13 \xleftarrow{\text{Divide by 2}} 26$$

The two operations used in making up the equation have to be 'undone' in the reverse order.

CLASSROOM ACTIVITY

Solving equations with a balance

You need a simple balance, of the type described in Section 5.3, p. 110 and a supply of identical small counters, such as bottle tops. Make these up into small packets which hide the number of counters inside. These packets can be labelled x, y, ... To illustrate the use of the balance consider the following example:

To solve $3x + 2 = 14$ (Solution $x = 4$)

1 Make up at least 3 x packets, each containing 4 counters.

2 Place the three x packets and 2 more counters in the left-hand scale pan (i.e. the pupils' left), and 14 counters in the right-hand pan; check that the beam of the balance is level.

3 Ask the class, 'If I take 2 counters out of the left-hand pan, what must I do to keep the pans balanced?' ('Take 2 out of the right-hand pan.') Remove the 2 from each pan, and check that they still balance.

4 'What equation does the balance now show?' ($3x = 12$). Write this equation on the board.

5 'There are three x's on the left; what can we do to leave just one of them?' (One possible answer is, 'Subtract two of them', but ask for another suggestion – 'Divide by 3'.) It could be helpful to lay the 3 x's and the 12 counters out in three rows.

6 Show that x balances with 4 counters. The packet can be opened to show that it does, indeed, contain 4 counters.

––––––––––––––––––– ◆ –––––––––––––––––––

The following solution procedure shows these steps clearly.

$$3x - 5 = 7 \qquad \text{Add 5}$$
$$3x \quad\;\; = 12 \qquad \text{Divide by 3}$$
$$x \quad\;\; = 4$$

Here, the 'wrapping up' operations on x to form the equation were:

First multiply by 3 to give $3x$, then subtract 5 which produces $(3x - 5)$.

To solve the equation these have to be undone in reverse order:

First add 5, then divide by 3.

3.73   Basic rules of number operations

Numbers can be added in any order:

$$3 + 8 + 5 = 8 + 3 + 5 = 5 + 8 + 3 = \ldots$$

The same is true of multiplication:

$$2 \times 7 \times 5 = 7 \times 5 \times 2 = 5 \times 7 \times 2 = \ldots$$

This is because the operations of addition (+) and multiplication (×) obey two fundamental principles or laws as they are sometimes known.

1 The *commutative law* tells us that, for any two numbers, the order in which they are combined does not matter:

$$a + b = b + a$$

and $\qquad\qquad a \times b = b \times a \quad$ or $\quad ab = ba$

2 *The associative law* tells us that, when we are adding or multiplying three or more numbers, it does not matter which pair we start with:

$$a + (b + c) = (a + b) + c$$

and $\qquad\qquad a \times (b \times c) = (a \times b) \times c$

a, b, c can stand for any numbers, and these statements are always true, whatever values a, b and c may have.

The same laws do not, however, apply to subtraction or division, as we have already seen. For example,

$$5 - 2 \neq 2 - 5, \quad 10 - (6 - 2) \neq (10 - 6) - 2$$
$$6 \div 3 \neq 3 \div 6, \quad 12 \div (6 \div 2) \neq (12 \div 6) \div 2$$

3 The last of the laws concerning operations is the *distributive law*, which we have seen is of basic importance in the multiplication algorithm (Section 3.55, p. 56). We say that *multiplication is distributive over addition and subtraction.*

$$a \times (b + c) = (a \times b) + (a \times c)$$
$$a \times (b - c) = (a \times b) - (a \times c)$$

Note that the names of these laws (commutative, associative, distributive) are not words to use with young pupils. They will accept the principles when carrying out computation, provided that they have been taught processes with understanding.

3.74   Zero and one

0 and 1 are the identities for addition and multiplication respectively:

$$a + 0 = a \quad \text{and} \quad a \times 1 = a$$

Also, 0 has an 'absorbent' effect in multiplication:

$$a \times 0 = 0, \quad 0 \times a = 0$$

Again, these are true whatever value a may have.

3.8   FACTORS, MULTIPLES AND DIVISIBILITY

3.81   Rectangular numbers

A number which is not prime has pairs of factors other than itself and 1. Such a number is said to be *composite*: its different factor pairs can be shown by rectangular arrays of small objects:

```
    *   *   *   *   *   *        *   *   *   *
    *   *   *   *   *   *        *   *   *   *
         12 = 2 × 6             *   *   *   *
                                  12 = 3 × 4
```

Pupils can experiment with different numbers of bottle tops or other counters, trying to make rectangular arrangements of them. With a prime number, they will only be able to arrange the counters in a single line – not in a rectangular pattern of 2 or more equal rows.

```
    *   *   *   *   *   *   *   *   *   *   *
```

Notice what happens when we try to arrange 11 objects in 2s, 3s, 4s, 5s . . . . :

```
*  *  *  *  *  *      *  *  *  *      *  *  *      *  *  *
*  *  *  *  *         *  *  *  *      *  *  *      *  *
                      *  *  *         *  *  *      *  *
                                      *  *         *  *
                                                   *  *
```

3.82   Divisibility tests

When trying to find factors, there are several simple tests which we can use before actually dividing. For example,

any multiple of 2 is an even number,

so we can see immediately whether 2 is a factor of a number or not depending on whether the units digit is even or odd (0 counts as even).

The multiples of 3 have a digital root of 3, 6 or 9: that is, when the digits of a multiple of 3 are added together, we obtain one of these numbers (3, 6, 9). For large numbers we may have to carry out this addition more than once, e.g.

$$372 \qquad 3 + 7 + 2 = 12 \qquad\qquad 1 + 2 = 3;$$

the digital root of 372 is 3.

$$56907 \qquad 5 + 6 + 9 + 0 + 7 = 27 \qquad 2 + 7 = 9;$$

the digital root of 56907 is 9.

$$42055 \qquad 4 + 2 + 0 + 5 + 5 = 16 \qquad 1 + 6 = 7;$$

the digital root of 42055 is 7.

So 372 and 56907 are both divisible by 3, but 42055 is not.

We have seen (Section 3.56, p. 59) that

multiples of 9 below 100 have a digital root of 9.

This is in fact true of all multiples of 9: this tells us that 56907 is divisible by 9.

Multiples of 5 are easily recognised, because

their units digit is either 5 or 0;

those ending in 0 are even, and therefore divisible by 2, and by 10 (2×5).

Multiples of 6 are multiples of both 2 and 3. To test whether a number is divisible by 6, therefore, apply both tests:

Is it even? Is its digital root 3, 6 or 9?

Referring to the examples above, therefore, 372 is a multiple of 6 but 56 907 is not.

There is no simple divisibility test for 7.

3.83   A pattern in subtraction

CLASSROOM ACTIVITY

Reversing digits

1   Ask each pupil to choose a 2-digit number, e.g. 25.

2   Tell the pupils to *reverse* the digits (52) and then to subtract the smaller number from the larger ($52 - 25 = 27$).

3 List the results of pupils on the blackboard, and ask the class,

'What do you notice about all of them?'
'Do you recognise them from the multiplication tables?'
'Which table do they all come in?' (They are all multiples of 9.)

4 Let pupils try some more examples to convince themselves that this is always true.

5 Repeat 1–3 for 3-digit numbers, e.g. 257, 752.

$$752 - 257 = 495$$

6 This time, ask pupils to check that their results are all divisible by 9, and to write them as a product,

e.g. $495 = 9 \times 55$

7 Write the products on the blackboard and ask, 'What do you notice about the other factor in each case?' (It is a multiple of 11.)

8 Let pupils try some more examples to convince themselves that this is always true.

———————————— ◆ ————————————

3.84 Common factors

We can list all the factors of a number by trial and error, dividing in turn by 2, 3, 4, 5, ... When we find a divisor which gives no remainder, then the divisor and quotient are one pair of factors. In this way, listing all the factors in order, we can pair them off from opposite ends. For example,

$$48 = 1 \times 48 = 2 \times 24 = 3 \times 16 = 4 \times 12 = 6 \times 8$$

so the complete list of factors of 48 is

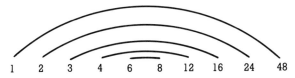

In the case of a square, there will be an unpaired factor in the middle: this is the *square root*. For instance, the factors of 64 are

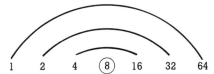

8 is the square root of 64.

It is then easy to see what factors two numbers have in common. The common factors of 48 and 64 are

$$1, \quad 2, \quad 4, \quad 8, \quad 16$$

and the last of these, 16, is the *highest common factor* (HCF) of the two numbers.

3.85 Common multiples

Numbers have a finite number of factors, but their multiples are infinite. For example, the multiples of 15 are

$$15, \quad 30, \quad 45, \quad 60, \quad 75, \quad 90, \quad 105, \quad \ldots$$

and there is no reason why we should ever stop this sequence. If we then write down the multiples of another number, 18 for example,

$$18, \quad 36, \quad 54, \quad 72, \quad 90, \quad 108, \quad 126, \quad \ldots$$

we may be able to see some common multiples in the lists, provided that they are long enough. Here, we can see that 90 is a common multiple of 15 and 18; in fact, it is the *lowest common multiple* (LCM). The next, as you can discover if you continue the lists, is 180, and the next 270.

Common multiples are important in work with fractions; when adding or subtracting fractions, the LCM of their denominators is the smallest denominator we can choose for their sum or difference (see Section 4.54, p. 89).

3.9 EXERCISES

1 Describe one method of teaching either addition or multiplication facts.

2 Describe one piece of apparatus which could be used to show a child that:
i) $77 + 9 = 86$
ii) $7 \times 12 = 84$.

Describe, with diagrams, exactly how the learning aid would be used for these calculations.

3 Describe in detail how to show, using either an abacus or place-value material, that
i) $478 - 254 = 224$
ii) $654 - 378 = 276$.

4 Describe how you would explain to a child that $24 \div 4 = 6$, using beans or other physical material,
i)   as a sharing situation
ii) as a repeated subtraction situation.

5 Draw arrow diagrams for wrapping and unwrapping to show the solutions of each of the following equations:

i) $2x - 5 = 35$
ii) $2(3x + 4) = 20$.

6 Complete the following identities correctly:

i) $a - b = \quad (b - a)$
ii) $a - (b - c) = (a - b)$

---◆---

3.91   Hints and answers

5 i)

ii)

6 i) $a - b = -(b - a)$
   ii) $a - (b - c) = (a - b) + c$

---◆---

CHAPTER FOUR

The Rational Numbers

4.1 INTRODUCTION

Rational numbers include fractions, which may be written as decimals, percentages and ratios. A rational number can always be written as the ratio of two whole numbers, e.g.

$$3 : 5 \quad 6 : 1 \quad 72 : 100 \quad 5 : 3$$

All of these can be written in different ways, e.g.

$$0.6 \quad 6 \quad 0.72 \quad 1.\dot{6}$$
$$60\% \quad 600\% \quad 72\% \quad 166\tfrac{2}{3}\%$$

but they are the same numbers.

4.2 CONCEPT OF FRACTIONS

When we divide an object, or a collection of objects, or a quantity of some kind, into any number of parts, then each part is called a *fraction* of the whole. (Fraction means something 'broken off'.) In order to give these fractions names, we need to make the division into *equal* parts.

There are many situations where children will meet fractions. We consider these under three headings:

Fractions of an object
Fractions of a collection
Fractions of a measured quantity.

4.21 Naming simple fractions with words

The observant teacher can find many examples of fractions occurring in everyday life and in the classroom. These should be named with spoken words before written symbols are introduced, and pupils' local language used if necessary to explain the English words.

Point out, to pupils, fractions of whole objects you might see in the classroom, e.g. half of a banana, a third of a stick, a quarter of a sheet of paper. Avoid referring to fractions whose whole part cannot be seen, such as one fifth of a litre of milk, one quarter of an hour: understanding of these will come later. Begin with *unit fractions* first – *one* half, *one* third, etc. Later introduce *two* thirds, *three* fifths, etc. Next introduce fractions of a collection of objects – half of a bunch of bananas, a quarter of a pile of 10 cent coins, a third of a group of children. Finally, when pupils have been introduced to the basic measurement concepts, introduce fractions such as half a pace, three quarters of the length of the room, one third of a bottle full.

4.22 Using diagrams

TEACHER DEMONSTRATION

1 The teacher folds a sheet of paper in half. Ask the class,

'Which half is bigger?' ('They are the same.')
'Can I make more than two halves?' ('No; there cannot be more than two halves.')

2 Fold another piece of paper, this time into quarters and ask the class,

'Which quarter is the biggest?' 'How many quarters are there?' etc.

3 Draw a large circle on the blackboard and divide it into six equal sectors. Ask similar questions about sixths.

———————◆———————

FOR THE TEACHER TO MAKE

A fraction disc

Materials required: a large square or rectangle of card; some sheets of plain white paper, smaller than the large card; a circular disc of coloured paper, smaller than the paper.

1 On each sheet of paper, draw a circle which is the same size as the disc. Using a protractor, or other means, divide one of the circles into 8 equal parts. (Other circles can be divided into 10, 12, 16 or more equal parts.) Later, write fractions round the edges of the circles as required (see Fig. 4.1).

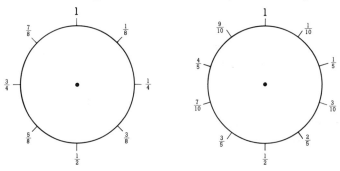

Fig. 4.1

2 Place one of the paper sheets in the middle of the large card. Carefully, cut a slit in the paper starting exactly at the centre of the circle, along a radius.

3 Cut an equal slit in exactly the same way in the card.

4 Cut along a radius of the coloured paper disc, exactly from the centre to the circumference. Insert the disc through the slits in the paper and card (see Fig. 4.2).

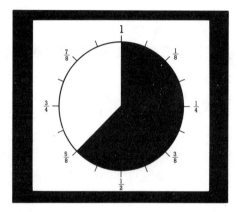

Fig. 4.2

Turn the disc against the paper. In this way, show different fractions of the circle drawn on the paper. Change to the other sheets of paper to show different fractions.

———————————— ◆ ————————————

4.3 INTRODUCING WRITTEN SYMBOLS

We write fractions using two whole numbers. The *denominator* (lower number) names the fraction – thirds, fifths, and so on. The *numerator* (upper number) tells us how many – *two* thirds, *four* fifths, and so on. The line or *bar* of the fraction is a kind of division sign; for example, $\frac{1}{4}$ shows us that a whole (1) has been divided into 4 equal parts.

4.31 Unit fractions

Introduce the written forms of fractions alongside diagrams starting with unit fractions (see Fig. 4.3).

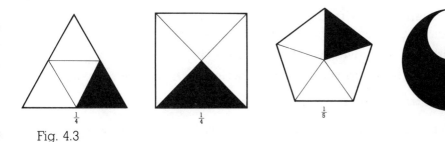

Fig. 4.3

4.32 Other fractions less than one

Progress to other fractions less than 1 (see Fig. 4.4).

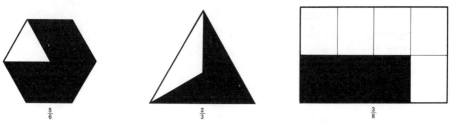

Fig. 4.4

Fractions can also be shown on a number line. For example, all the fifths between 0 and 1 can be marked, equally spaced, along a line.

4.33 Fractions greater than one (improper fractions)

Divide two discs each into quarters; with eight quarters we can have

$$\tfrac{3}{4} \quad \text{or} \quad \tfrac{4}{4} \quad \text{or} \quad \tfrac{5}{4} \quad \text{or} \quad \tfrac{6}{4} \quad \ldots$$

In fact, we can have any number of quarters if we start with more than a single 'whole', provided that these 'wholes' are all the same. Fractions which have a numerator greater than the denominator are called *improper*.

Since 4 quarters are the same as 1 whole,

$$\tfrac{4}{4} = 1, \qquad \tfrac{5}{4} = \tfrac{4}{4} + \tfrac{1}{4} = 1 + \tfrac{1}{4} \text{ (written as } 1\tfrac{1}{4})$$
$$\tfrac{7}{4} = \tfrac{4}{4} + \tfrac{3}{4} = 1 + \tfrac{3}{4} \text{ or } 1\tfrac{3}{4}$$
$$\tfrac{8}{4} = \tfrac{4}{4} + \tfrac{4}{4} = 2$$

In this way, we can write an improper fraction as a *mixed number* – the sum of a whole number and a *proper* fraction. Note that we do not write a + sign between the whole number and the fraction. As shown above, the improper fraction $\tfrac{7}{4}$ is equal to the mixed number $1\tfrac{3}{4}$.

We usually think of fractions as smaller than a whole, but dividing any number by another gives a fraction of some kind, e.g.

dividing 2 by 3 gives two thirds : $2 \div 3 = \frac{2}{3}$,

dividing 5 by 3 gives the improper fraction $\frac{5}{3}$, which is the same as $1\frac{2}{3}$.

Improper fractions or mixed numbers can be shown on the number line.

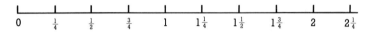

4.4 EQUIVALENT FRACTIONS

One of the most important ideas in fraction work is the concept of *equivalence*. Equivalent fractions have the same *value*, and therefore appear in the same place on the number line.

LESSON ACTIVITY

Pupils can work in small groups ; each group should have a few sheets of paper (which could be half-used), all the same size. The teacher should demonstrate each step to the class using, if possible, large sheets.

1 Take one sheet of paper and tear it exactly into halves. Take another sheet of the same size, and tear it into quarters. On the clean side of each piece, write the fraction of the whole ($\frac{1}{2}$ or $\frac{1}{4}$).

2 Place the quarters on top of the halves, to show that two quarters are the same as one half.

3 On squared paper, each pupil should draw a rectangle, eight units long by six units wide. They should divide it into eight and then, using coloured pencils, or different kinds of shading complete a diagram like Fig. 4.5.

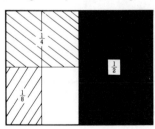

Fig. 4.5

Ask pupils to complete the following below the diagram :

$$\frac{1}{2} = \frac{}{4} = \frac{}{8} \qquad \frac{1}{4} = \frac{}{8} \qquad \frac{3}{4} = \frac{}{8}$$

Note that the same size of rectangle, 8×6, can be divided equally into 3, 6 and 12 parts. Similar diagrams can then be drawn and shaded to show, for example,

$$\frac{1}{2} = \frac{3}{6} = \frac{6}{12} \qquad \frac{1}{3} = \frac{2}{6} = \frac{4}{12} \qquad \frac{2}{3} = \frac{4}{6} = \frac{8}{12}$$

◆

FOR THE TEACHER TO MAKE

A fraction board/chart

A large fraction board is needed for classroom use, but pupils can later draw their own charts on squared exercise book paper.

1 Draw a long thin rectangle; the ideal length is 60 units, and the breadth should be about 5 units.

2 Draw a series of equal rectangles below this, six or seven at least.

3 Divide the second rectangle into two halves, the next into three thirds, the next four quarters, and so on. (7ths, 9ths and 11ths could be omitted; they are difficult to draw accurately, and are less commonly used.) A complete chart is shown in Fig. 4.6.

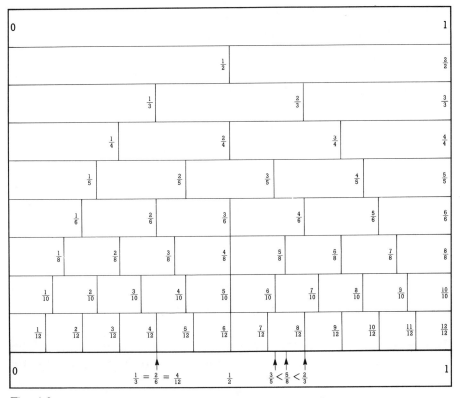

Fig. 4.6

◆

Use the fraction board to show

a) Equivalence, e.g. $\frac{1}{3} = \frac{2}{6} = \frac{4}{12}$
b) The order of size of fractions, e.g. $\frac{3}{5} < \frac{5}{8} < \frac{2}{3}$

Pupils must know that they can multiply, or divide, both the top and bottom numbers of a fraction by a common factor, and the value of the fraction will not change.

The teacher should stress certain equivalent fractions as preparation for decimal work, e.g.

$$\frac{3}{5} = \frac{6}{10}, \quad \frac{7}{20} = \frac{35}{100}$$

4.5 DECIMAL NOTATION

4.51 Extending the place-value system

Pupils should notice what happens when we divide by ten:

$$1300 \div 10 = 130 \quad = 1 \text{ hundred} + 3 \text{ tens}$$

$$130 \div 10 = \quad 13 \quad = 1 \text{ ten} \qquad + 3 \text{ units}$$

$$13 \div 10 = \quad 1\tfrac{3}{10} = 1 \text{ unit} \qquad + 3 \text{ tenths}$$

the digits move one place to the right. Decimal notation extends the place-value system further to the right. Instead of writing the fraction in the last line above, we write the 3 in a new *tenths* column, to the right of the *units* column. But, to show that we have gone past the units place, we write a point, or in some countries a comma, to separate the whole number from the fraction, i.e. 1.3.

Look at another example:

$$2580 \quad \div 10 = 258$$

$$258 \quad \div 10 = \quad 25.8$$

$$25.8 \div 10 = \quad 2.58$$

The 2 represents 2 *thousands* first, then 2 *hundreds*, then 2 *tens* and then 2 *units*; each division by 10 carries it one place to the right. In the same way, the 8 represents, successively, 8 *tens*, 8 *units*, 8 *tenths*, and 8 *hundredths*.

Examples likes these can be shown to a class using a *place-value chart*.

Fig. 4.7

This consists of a sheet of card labelled as shown in Fig. 4.7 with slits to hold different numeral cards. Cards can be tapered to slot in easily and a large, black-painted drawing pin can represent the decimal point. A second sheet of card can be stuck carefully behind the first to keep cards in place.

4.52 Representing two decimal places

1 Currency often provides a good introduction to hundredths. For example, a dollar is made up from 100 cents, so $1 \text{ c} = \$ 0.01$. Pupils should learn to record sums of money in two different ways, i.e. using both units, and using the large one only, with decimal notation:

$$\$ 3 \ 35 \text{ c} = \$ 3.35$$

2 On squared exercise book paper (or 5 mm ruling graph paper), draw a 10×10 square to represent a unit. Tenths are shown as 1×10 strips and hundredths as single cells. Fig. 4.8 shows the number 2.68.

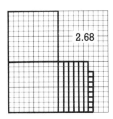

Fig. 4.8

3 1 metre = 100 cm. A metre rule with every centimetre marked serves as a number line from 0 to 1 with every 100th shown. Pupils can measure their own heights and learn to record them in three different ways:

$$147 \text{ cm} = 1 \text{ m } 47 \text{ cm} = 1.47 \text{ m}$$

Note With currency, the convention is to write the large unit on the left of the whole number (see (1) above), but with units of measure the unit symbol is always written to the right of the digits, even when they include decimal places.

4.53 Decimals on the number line – the rational numbers

As mentioned in the introduction, a rational number can always be written as the ratio of two whole numbers. The rational numbers help to fill the gaps between whole numbers on a number line; there is no end to this filling-in process. For example, the segment of number line from 2 to 3 can first be enlarged to show tenths.

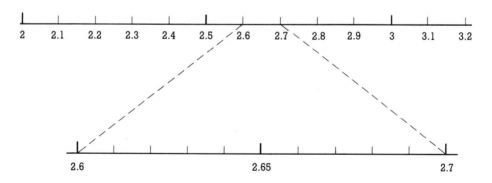

A portion from 2.6 to 2.7 is enlarged to show hundredths. Enlarging again, we could show thousandths (3 decimal places), and then numbers with 4, 5, 6, . . . decimal places.

Using a number line, pupils can learn to place decimals in order, e.g. 2.1, 2.05, 2.25, 2.205 appear on a line like this:

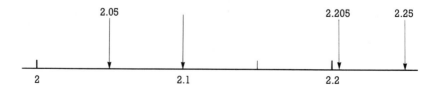

4.54 **Writing decimals as fractions**

Pupils should understand that tenths and hundredths can be written either as a decimal – 0.3, 0.47 – or as a fraction – $\frac{3}{10}$, $\frac{47}{100}$. It is, therefore, easy to rewrite a decimal as a fraction. It may often be possible to rewrite this fraction in *lower terms*, as an equivalent fraction using smaller numbers. For example,

$$0.6 = \frac{6}{10} = \frac{3}{5} \qquad 0.45 = \frac{45}{100} = \frac{9}{20}$$

Notice that the only factors of 100 are 2, 4, 5, 10, 20, 25, 50. Only fractions which have one of these numbers as denominator will give 2-place decimals, e.g.

$$\frac{3}{4} = \frac{3 \times 25}{4 \times 25} = \frac{75}{100} = 0.75 \qquad \frac{2}{5} = \frac{2 \times 2}{5 \times 2} = \frac{4}{10} = 0.4$$

4.55 **Percentages**

A percentage is simply a number of *hundredths*. If a pupil scores 73% in a test, then he has $\frac{73}{100}$ of the total mark. So a percentage can be expressed in three equivalent ways:

$$81\% = \frac{81}{100} = 0.81 \qquad 5\% = \frac{5}{100} = 0.05$$

The per cent symbol, %, is another way of writing 'over 100'. The teacher should stress these equivalent forms when introducing percentages, and whenever the opportunity arises.

Expressing a fraction as a percentage involves writing the fraction as a decimal, then multiplying by 100% (i.e. 100 'over' 100), e.g.

$$\frac{3}{5} = 0.6 = 0.6 \times \frac{100}{100} = \frac{60}{100} = 60\%$$

4.56 **Writing fractions as decimals**

Some fractions can be expressed directly as equivalent fractions with denominator 10, 100, or 1000, . . . These fractions can therefore be written as terminating decimals; that is, they end after 1, 2, 3, . . . decimal places. For example,

$$\frac{3}{5} = \frac{6}{10} = 0.6 \qquad \frac{9}{20} = \frac{45}{100} = 0.45 \qquad \frac{5}{8} = \frac{5 \times 125}{8 \times 125} = \frac{625}{1000} = 0.625$$

Other fractions have denominators which cannot be multiplied by any factor to give a power of 10. For these, the only way to proceed is to divide the numerator by the denominator – remember that the 'line' of a fraction is like a division sign (see Section 4.3, p. 78). This method works for any denominator, e.g.

$$
\begin{array}{r}
0.625 \\
\hline
8\,|\,5.000 \\
4\ 8 \\
\hline
20 \\
16 \\
\hline
40 \\
40 \\
\hline
\end{array}
$$

Note that the decimal point falls into place in the quotient as we reach it in the dividend. Give pupils examples of such divisions which terminate and insist on clear layout, with special care in the vertical alignment of the places. They should obtain each of the quarters $(\frac{1}{4}, \frac{3}{4})$ and eighths $(\frac{1}{8}, \frac{3}{8}, \frac{5}{8}, \frac{7}{8})$ in this way.

Notice, however, what happens when the divisor does not 'go' exactly, e.g. for $\frac{5}{6}$ and $\frac{3}{11}$:

$$
\begin{array}{r}
0.833\ldots \\
\hline
6\,|\,5.0000\ldots \\
4\ 8 \\
\hline
20 \\
18 \\
\hline
20 \\
18 \\
\hline
20 \\
\end{array}
\qquad
\begin{array}{r}
0.2727\ldots \\
\hline
11\,|\,3.0000\ldots \\
2.2 \\
\hline
80 \\
77 \\
\hline
30 \\
22 \\
\hline
80 \\
77 \\
\hline
30 \\
\end{array}
$$

After a while, the same remainders appear over and over again; this leads to *recurring* digits in the quotient. Such recurring decimals never terminate, and so we write them in a shorthand form:

$$\tfrac{5}{6} = 0.8333\ldots = 0.8\dot{3} \qquad \tfrac{3}{11} = 0.272727\ldots = 0.\dot{2}\dot{7}$$

In the first of these, the single dot shows that the 3 recurs, after the initial 8 (0.8333 . . .). In the second, the two dots show that both digits recur

(0.272727 . . .). When there are more than two recurring digits, we write a dot over the first and last, e.g.

$$\tfrac{4}{7} = 0.\dot{5}7142\dot{8} \quad (= 0.57142857142857 \ldots)$$

The only recurring decimals which pupils need to meet at first are those for $\tfrac{1}{3}$ and $\tfrac{2}{3}$. These can both be found using the division method; point out to pupils that, at each step in the division, the remainder is the same:

$$\begin{array}{c} 0.3\ 3\ 3\ \ldots \\ \hline 3\,\big|\,1.0^10^10 \ldots \end{array} \qquad \begin{array}{c} 0.6\ 6\ 6 \ldots \\ \hline 3\,\big|\,2.0^20^20 \ldots \end{array}$$

4.57   Arranging fractions in order

In some cases, we can tell which of two fractions is the larger immediately. With unit fractions the larger denominator means the smaller fraction. Comparing $\tfrac{1}{5}$ with $\tfrac{1}{3}$, $5 > 3$, so 5 divides 1 into more parts than 3 does. Therefore, $\tfrac{1}{5}$ is smaller than $\tfrac{1}{3}$.

In other cases, pupils may remember from diagrams such as those in Section 4.2 that, for example, $\tfrac{3}{4} < \tfrac{4}{5}$:

The simplest way to decide which of two fractions is the larger is to rewrite them as decimals, e.g.

$$\tfrac{5}{8} = 0.625, \quad \tfrac{3}{5} = 0.6, \quad \text{so} \ \tfrac{5}{8} > \tfrac{3}{5}$$

4.6   ADDITION AND SUBTRACTION OF FRACTIONS

4.61   Fractions with the same denominator

An oral explanation is often helpful here: '*Three* eighths plus *two* eighths equals *five* eighths', just as three beans plus two beans equals five beans. Relate this to the written form:

$$\frac{3}{8} + \frac{2}{8} = \frac{5}{8}$$

At this stage it is better to avoid using a 'long line' $\left(\dfrac{3+2}{8}\right)$ which may

confuse the pupil. Rectangular and circular diagrams can help the understanding (see Fig. 4.9, overleaf).

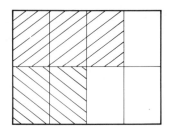

Fig. 4.9

4.62 One denominator a multiple of the other

When one denominator is a multiple of the other, we can say that the fractions belong to the same family: 10 is a multiple of 5, so $\frac{2}{5}$ and $\frac{3}{10}$ belong to the same family. Write the fraction with the smaller denominator in its equivalent form with the larger one:

$$\frac{2}{5} + \frac{3}{10} = \frac{4}{10} + \frac{3}{10} = \frac{7}{10}$$

4.63 Mixed numbers

Add or subtract the whole number parts first, then the fractional parts:

$$1\tfrac{1}{5} + 3\tfrac{2}{5} = 1 + \frac{1}{5} + 3 + \frac{2}{5} = (1 + 3) + \left(\frac{1}{5} + \frac{2}{5}\right) = 4\tfrac{3}{5}$$

If the sum of the fractional parts is more than 1, then regroup accordingly:

$$2\tfrac{2}{3} + 4\tfrac{2}{3} = (2 + 4) + \left(\frac{2}{3} + \frac{2}{3}\right) = 6 + \frac{4}{3} = 6 + 1\tfrac{1}{3} = 7\tfrac{1}{3}$$

Where possible, express the final fraction in its lowest terms:

$$2\tfrac{5}{8} + 1\tfrac{7}{8} = 3 + \frac{12}{8} = 3 + 1\tfrac{4}{8} = 4\tfrac{4}{8} = 4\tfrac{1}{2}$$

When the fractional part to be *subtracted* is the larger, 'decompose' one unit into a suitable fraction:

$$1 - \frac{5}{12} = \frac{12}{12} - \frac{5}{12} = \frac{7}{12}$$

$$14\tfrac{3}{8} - 3\tfrac{5}{8} = (13 + 1\tfrac{3}{8}) - 3\tfrac{5}{8} = 13\tfrac{11}{8} - 3\tfrac{5}{8} = 10\tfrac{6}{8} = 10\tfrac{3}{4}$$

4.64 Fractions with different denominators

In general, we must rewrite both fractions as equivalent ones with the same denominator. First, find a suitable common denominator: once this has been done the calculation can proceed. Note that the common denominator can be any common multiple (see Section 3.85, p. 74) of the separate denominators, but we normally choose the smallest or lowest common multiple, the LCM.

$$\frac{2}{3}+\frac{4}{5} = \frac{10}{15}+\frac{12}{15} = \frac{22}{15} = 1\frac{7}{15} \quad (3 \text{ and } 5 \text{ have LCM } 15)$$

$$1\frac{1}{4}-\frac{5}{6} = 1\frac{3}{12}-\frac{10}{12} = \frac{15}{12}-\frac{10}{12} = \frac{5}{12} \quad (4 \text{ and } 6 \text{ have LCM } 12)$$

4.7 OPERATIONS WITH DECIMALS

4.71 Addition and subtraction

All decimals can be linked to their fraction equivalents, e.g.

$$0.3 + 0.4 = \tfrac{3}{10} + \tfrac{4}{10} = \tfrac{7}{10} = 0.7$$

Examples can be illustrated on squared paper (see Section 4.52).

The algorithms for addition and subtraction of decimals are the same as those for whole numbers, but take care to align the digit places correctly, e.g.

$$2.45 + 3.7 \qquad \begin{array}{r} 2.45 \\ + 3.7 \\ \hline 6.15 \end{array} \qquad 5.2 - 2.45 \qquad \begin{array}{r} 5.20 \\ - 2.45 \\ \hline 2.75 \end{array}$$

The zero can be written in the second example to keep the subtraction like that of whole numbers.

4.72 Multiplying and dividing by a whole number

The number line can be used to illustrate simple examples, as with whole numbers, e.g. 3×0.4 (3 lots of 0.4) ($= 1.2$):

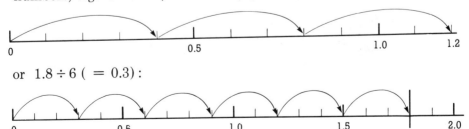

or $1.8 \div 6$ ($= 0.3$):

Again, the algorithms are the same as those for whole numbers. The decimal point falls into place as it is reached:

$$3.65 \times 4 \qquad \begin{array}{r} 3.65 \\ \times\ 4 \\ \hline 14.60 \end{array} \qquad 14.8 \div 4 \qquad \begin{array}{r} 3.7 \\ 4\overline{\smash{)}14.8} \end{array}$$

Final zeros should always be written at first: they can be dropped or ignored later.

All this work can be made practical by reference to sums of money, to lengths or other metric measures.

At first, examples of division should terminate, or 'go exactly', but some may extend the quotient to 1 or 2 extra places:

$$22.5 \div 6 \qquad \begin{array}{r} 3.75 \\ 6\overline{\smash{)}22.50} \end{array}$$

Much later, pupils can be introduced to the idea of rounding, but this depends on an understanding of approximations.

4.8 MULTIPLICATION

4.81 Multiplication of fractions

When a fraction is multiplied by a whole number, we can illustrate it with a diagram, e.g.

$$5 \times \tfrac{3}{4} = 3\tfrac{3}{4}$$

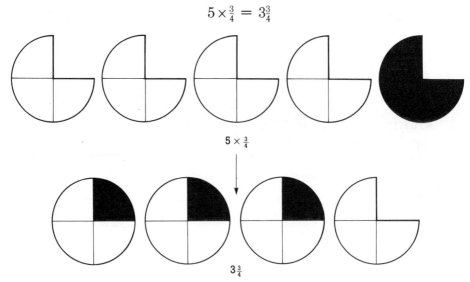

Fig. 4.10

The 'reverse' product – fraction × whole number – is harder to under-stand; but pupils may understand that the word 'of' means the same as 'times' in this context:

$$3 \text{ lots of } 5 = 3 \times 5$$

$$1 \text{ lot of } 5 = 1 \times 5$$

$$\tfrac{3}{4} \text{ of } 5 = \tfrac{3}{4} \times 5$$

Pupils know that multiplication of whole numbers is commutative (see Section 3.53, p. 55), so it should not surprise them that, for example,

$$5 \times \tfrac{3}{4} = \tfrac{3}{4} \times 5$$

Multiplication of whole numbers can be shown by area diagrams, multiplying length and breadth: 3×4 is seen in Fig. 4.11a. Similarly, a product of fractions can be shown: $\tfrac{2}{3} \times \tfrac{4}{5}$ is illustrated in Fig. 4.11b.

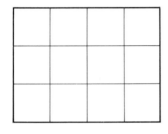
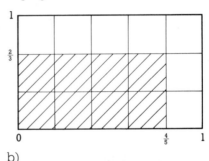

Fig. 4.11   a)   b)

In multiplying thirds by fifths, the diagram shows that the product will be a number of fifteenths, because the rectangle is divided into 3×5 equal cells. We can also see how the product of the numerators gives the number of fifteenths, leading to the general method:

$$\frac{2}{3} \times \frac{4}{5} = \frac{2 \times 4}{3 \times 5} = \frac{8}{15}$$

Note that we can also regard this as $\tfrac{2}{3}$ of $\tfrac{4}{5}$ (see Fig. 4.12): the area shaded ▨ is $\tfrac{4}{5}$ of the unit, and the part shaded ▨ is $\tfrac{2}{3}$ of this.

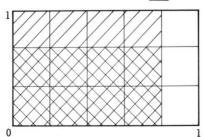

Fig. 4.12

The kind of diagram shown in Fig. 4.11b can be used with numbers greater than 1, e.g. $1\frac{3}{5} \times 1\frac{3}{4}$ (see Fig. 4.13). We can see how it is best to write these mixed numbers as improper fractions; in the figure, the sides of the area concerned have lengths $\frac{8}{5}$ and $\frac{7}{4}$. After one or two examples of this kind, pupils should be able to use the general procedure with understanding.

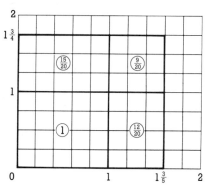

Fig. 4.13

In drawing diagrams like these, the basic unit does not need to be a square – rectangles serve just as well. The teacher needs to present one with dimensions which 'fit' the fractions in the product, e.g. thirds need a length which is a multiple of 3.

4.82 Multiplication of decimals

Start by writing decimals as fractions:

$$0.4 \times 0.3 = \frac{4}{10} \times \frac{3}{10} = \frac{12}{100} = 0.12$$

Again, this is well illustrated by an area diagram (see Fig. 4.14).

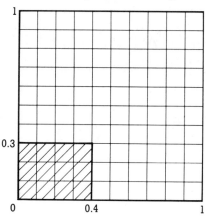

Fig. 4.14

Extend this gradually to numbers greater than 1, and to 2 or 3 decimal places, e.g.

$$1.4 \times 0.32 = 1\tfrac{4}{10} \times \frac{32}{100} = \frac{14 \times 32}{10 \times 100} = \frac{448}{1000} = 0.448$$

The rule about decimal places is then clear: the number of places in the product is the sum of those in the two factors. Care is needed when the product ends in zeros, e.g.

$$2.5 \times 1.2 = \frac{25}{10} \times \frac{12}{10} = 3.00, \text{ or simply } 3$$

Confident pupils can verify examples like the last by thinking partly in fractions.

$$2\tfrac{1}{2} \times 1.2 = 2 \times 1.2 + \frac{1}{2} \text{ of } 1.2 = 2.4 + 0.6 = 3$$

After simple examples, use the more general method, multiplying the digits and inserting the decimal point correctly afterwards. Encourage rough estimates, e.g.

12.3×2.8 will be about 30;

this will help pupils to check the position of the decimal point, that this is about 30, not 3 or 300.

4.9 DIVISION

Division of one fraction by another and of two decimal numbers should be restricted to simple cases arising from practical situations. This section shows how the concept of division can be introduced.

4.91 Dividing a whole number by a fraction

Start with division by a unit fraction, e.g. $4 \div \tfrac{1}{3}$. This can be thought of as a repeated subtraction: 'How many $\tfrac{1}{3}$s are there in 4?' We can show this on a number line:

There are 12 $\tfrac{1}{3}$s in 4.

After several such examples, point out to pupils that

$$4 \div \frac{1}{3} = 4 \times 3$$

$$3 \div \frac{1}{5} = 3 \times 5, \quad \text{etc.}$$

Extend this to division by more general fractions, but make sure that the quotient is a whole number, e.g. $6 \div \frac{3}{4} = 8$ (there are eight $\frac{3}{4}$s in 6):

4.92 Dividing a fraction by a whole number

Once again, area diagrams show why, for example, dividing $\frac{2}{5}$ by 3 will first give an answer in 15ths (see Fig. 4.15):

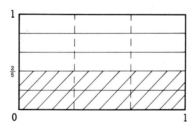

Fig. 4.15

This is the sharing aspect of division – $\frac{2}{5}$ shared between 3 is $\frac{2}{15}$.

Again, after several examples pupils should note that

$$\frac{2}{5} \div 3 = \frac{2}{5} \times \frac{1}{3}$$

$$\frac{3}{4} \div 6 = \frac{3}{4} \times \frac{1}{6}, \quad \text{etc.}$$

They should discover for themselves that dividing by one number gives the same result as multiplying by its *reciprocal*, or '1 over' the number.

4.93 **Dividing one fraction by another**

Neither of the previous methods provides a suitable model in the general case. All further work on division, of fractions and of decimals, depends on the concept of equivalence. For fractions we can write the divisions as 'double decker' fractions, e.g.

$$\frac{1}{3} \div \frac{1}{2} = \frac{\frac{1}{3}}{\frac{1}{2}}$$

Make the denominator 1 by multiplying top and bottom by 2:

$$\frac{\frac{1}{3}}{\frac{1}{2}} = \frac{\frac{1}{3} \times 2}{\frac{1}{2} \times 2} = \frac{\frac{2}{3}}{1} = \frac{2}{3}$$

4.94 **Division of decimals**

This depends on equivalent fractions, or divisions; the aim is always to 'make the divisor (denominator) a whole number', e.g.

$$2.35 \div 0.4 = \frac{2.35}{0.4} = \frac{23.5}{4}$$

$$0.216 \div 7.2 = \frac{0.216}{7.2} = \frac{2.16}{72}$$

It is helpful to write the division as a fraction, with the digits arranged vertically according to their place value, as shown above.

4.10 **EXERCISES**

1 Explain as clearly as possible, using diagrams and words, which is the larger fraction in each of the following pairs

i) $\frac{1}{3}$ and $\frac{1}{5}$

ii) $\frac{2}{5}$ and $\frac{4}{5}$

iii) $\frac{4}{5}$ and $\frac{3}{4}$

iv) $\frac{5}{7}$ and $\frac{2}{3}$

2 Using simple fractions, and diagrams which show them, make a set of fraction matching cards for a snap game (see Section 2.6, p. 20).

3 Make a set of either matching cards or domino cards to reinforce equivalence. Use all the fractions with denominators 2, 3, 4, 6 and 8, including those which are not in their lowest terms.

4 Use a number line to explain the following method of subtraction, which is a form of *complementary addition* (see Section 3.47, p. 52):

$$3\tfrac{1}{5} - 1\tfrac{3}{4} = 2 - 1\tfrac{3}{4} + 1\tfrac{1}{5} = \tfrac{1}{4} + 1\tfrac{1}{5} = 1\tfrac{9}{20}$$

5 Use an *equal additions* technique (see Section 3.47, p. 52) to work out the following subtraction:

$5\tfrac{1}{4} - 2\tfrac{5}{8}$ (Add 1 (unit) to one number, and 8 eighths to the other.)

Now use the same technique to work out

$$4\tfrac{2}{3} - 1\tfrac{3}{4}$$

6 Draw a circle and divide it into 10 equal sectors with radii spaced at 36° intervals. How would you use this to show that 45% of a class are boys and 55% girls?

7 Draw diagrams (number lines or shapes divided into parts) to illustrate the following:

i) $4\tfrac{1}{2} \div \tfrac{3}{4}$

ii) $3\tfrac{1}{4} \div \tfrac{1}{2}$

iii) $4\tfrac{1}{4} \div \tfrac{3}{4}$

8 Show $\tfrac{2}{5} \div \tfrac{3}{4} = \tfrac{2}{5} \times \tfrac{4}{3}$

———————————— ◆ ————————————

4.91 Hints and answers

1 i)   Sharing a dish of food equally between 3 people means that they will each have a larger helping than if there were 5 people.

ii)   Link this to the language, e.g. 'Here we have 2 fifths, ... and there we have 4 fifths – there are more fifths here than there'.

iii) $\tfrac{4}{5}$ needs $\tfrac{1}{5}$ to make it 1 ; $\tfrac{3}{4}$ needs $\tfrac{1}{4}$ to make it 1. $\tfrac{4}{5}$ is closer to 1. Support this with a diagram or number line.

2 Cards could show the same fraction in different ways, (see Fig. 4.16).

Fig. 4.16

4 $1\tfrac{3}{4}$ needs $\tfrac{1}{4}$ to make it up to 2 ; from 2 to $3\tfrac{1}{5}$ is $1\tfrac{1}{5}$.

5 $5\tfrac{1}{4} - 2\tfrac{5}{8} = 5\tfrac{10}{8} - 3\tfrac{5}{8}$; $4\tfrac{2}{3} - 1\tfrac{3}{4} = 4\tfrac{20}{12} - 2\tfrac{9}{12}$

6

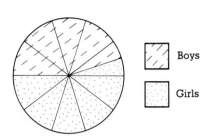

Boys

Girls

7 i)

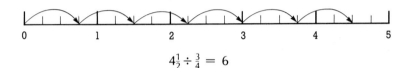

$$4\frac{1}{2} \div \frac{3}{4} = 6$$

ii) $\frac{1}{2}$ 'goes into 3' 6 times; the 'remainder' of $\frac{1}{4}$ is half the divisor $\frac{1}{2}$. So the quotient is $6\frac{1}{2}$.

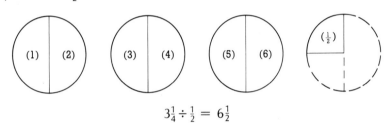

$$3\frac{1}{4} \div \frac{1}{2} = 6\frac{1}{2}$$

iii) Here the 'remainder', $\frac{1}{2}$, is $\frac{2}{3}$ of the divisor $\frac{3}{4}$. The quotient is therefore $5\frac{2}{3}$.

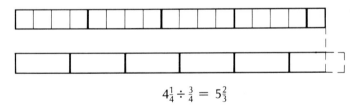

$$4\frac{1}{4} \div \frac{3}{4} = 5\frac{2}{3}$$

8 $\dfrac{\frac{2}{5}}{\frac{3}{4}} = \dfrac{\frac{2}{5} \times \frac{4}{3}}{\frac{3}{4} \times \frac{4}{3}} = \dfrac{\frac{2}{5} \times \frac{4}{3}}{1} = \frac{2}{5} \times \frac{4}{3}$

CHAPTER FIVE

Length, Mass, Capacity

5.1 INTRODUCTION

Measurement is an important application of mathematics. In school it should arise, if possible, from simple practical situations; it can then be one of the most interesting topics for both pupil and teacher.

5.11 Aims of teaching measurement

Teaching should equip the school leaver to:

1 Know and use the standard common measures

2 Estimate quantities sensibly, using appropriate units

3 Measure length, mass ('weight'), volume and capacity, area, time, angle and temperature to a realistic degree of accuracy

4 Carry out basic calculations with such measures as arise in practical, everyday situations.

5.12 Nature of measurement

In measuring we compare objects or quantities with others of known size. Children's ideas of length, mass, capacity and so on develop in stages. We can compare two table lengths *directly*, placing them side by side; if this is not convenient, use a third object, such as a stick, as a 'go-between'. Take it to each table in turn, mark the stick in different places, and find out which table is longer – this is *indirect* comparison.

Similarly, compare the masses of two bricks by placing them on the pans of a balance, and the capacities of two containers by filling one and pouring its contents into the other: these are *direct* comparisons. But if we fill both containers and pour the contents in turn into a third, larger container, then we are comparing their capacities *indirectly*. In none of these examples, however, do we need to *quantify* the amounts.

We can choose a much smaller *unit* – a stick length, the mass of coin, or the capacity of a spoon – to quantify the amounts compared assigning a *number of units* to each one. However, sticks, coins and spoonfuls are not the same everywhere, so the need arose to establish *standard units* for everyone in a community to use. For length, body units – handspans, feet, paces, the biblical cubit (distance from elbow to fingertip) – were widely used in the past, but even these were not standard for everyone. Different nations adopted different standard units but, with the growth of international trade, one system has come to dominate the world: the *metric* system of units.

5.13 Developing aspects of measurement

In all branches of measurement, we can identify the following teaching stages:

1 Language and vocabulary used in comparing and measuring

2 Conservation – understanding a quantity does not change its length, mass or capacity

3 Comparison:
  a) Directly
  b) Indirectly, using another object as an intermediary

4 Using non-standard or *arbitrary* units

5 Using standard units (usually metric) and knowing the relationships between them; estimation

6 Accurate measurement, using calibrated scales and instruments

7 Problem solving (oral and written) involving use of units, including the use of fractions and decimals.

The last of these stages often dominates classroom work. However, it is very important that children form clear concepts by careful progression through the earlier stages of measurement experiencing a variety of practical activities.

Two further general skills are essential if a pupil is to measure proficiently (see (6) above):

a) Ability to read a scale, interpolating or rounding to the nearest scale mark as appropriate

b) Ability to approximate numbers and quantities, whether large or small.

A child's readiness for a new stage depends on the individual, and will vary from one branch of measurement to another. Much depends on the opportunities for practical work which the teacher can create. Some concepts are harder to grasp than others: for example, an understanding of *length* is generally acquired sooner than a comparable understanding of *time*. In this way the development of one branch of measurement may lag behind another, but pupils must not be rushed through the early stages.

We now deal with the development of length, mass and capacity where there are clear similarities at each stage.

5.2 LENGTH

5.21 Language and vocabulary
Draw pupils' attention to the length properties of objects:

'Look at this boy; he is *tall*.'
'That table is *long*.'
'This bench is *narrow*.'

Ask children to describe objects:

'What can you say about this stick? ... And this one?'

and later ask them to show a length:

'Show me the *width* of the room.'
'Where is Kwame's *height*?'

As the concepts develop, so children need a vocabulary for length:

Long (longer, longest), short (shorter, shortest), wide (wider, widest), narrow (narrower, narrowest), tall (taller, tallest).
Length, breadth, width, height, depth, distance between/along.
High, low, near, far, thick, thin.

5.22 Conservation of length
The length of an object does not change when it is put in a different position.

Rigid objects
Show two sticks of the same length to a child, and ask, 'Are they the same length?' Then turn one of the sticks and ask, 'Are they still the same length?'

Flexible objects
Show the child two identical pieces of string. Move one of them, making it into a different shape, and ask, 'Which piece is longer?'

5.23 Comparison

Comparing two similar objects

Simple visual situations lead to questions such as:

'Which table is the longer one?'
'Which is the taller child?'
'Which piece of string is the shorter one?'
'Which edges of the page are the longer ones?'

Comparison and ordering of more than two lengths

Organise some activities for children, individually or in small groups:

Arrange three pencils in order: which is the shortest?
Arrange a group of four children in order of height: who is the tallest?
Who is the next tallest?

In these activities, lengths are compared *directly*. This may be developed using a specially prepared set of objects. For example, give children the experience of comparing lengths and breadths of rectangles which have been carefully designed to draw out different comparisons.

CLASS ACTIVITY

Lengths and breadths of rectangles

Teacher's preparation

1 On a sheet of A4 paper, draw a set of rectangles as shown in Fig. 5.1 (measurements given in cm) all of them having different lengths and breadths.

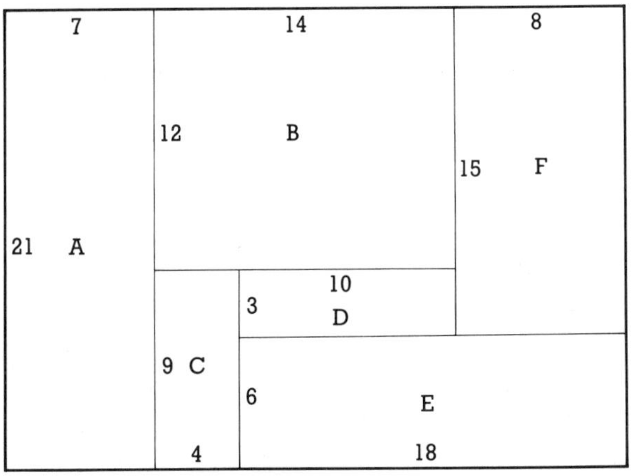

Fig. 5.1

2 Glue the sheet to a piece of card.

3 Cut out the rectangles, and letter them A, B, C, etc.

Note. A complete set of rectangles will be needed by each group of children; such a group should not contain more than six children.

Group activities

a) Identify the *length* and the *breadth* (or *width*) of each rectangle in turn.
b) Arrange the rectangles in order of length, from the longest to the shortest.
c) Arrange them in order of breadth, from the broadest to the narrowest.
d) Find two rectangles where the longer one is also the broader (e.g. A and E).
e) Find two rectangles where the longer one is the narrower (e.g. E and F).
f) Find a set of three (or more) rectangles which get narrower as they get shorter (e.g. A, E and C).
g) Find a set of three (or more) which get broader as they get shorter (e.g. A, F and B).

Individual work

From a double page of squared exercise book paper, children should draw (using a ruler) and cut out rectangles which illustrate relationships like those above. They should paste these in their exercise books and write sentences about them.

------------------------ ◆ ------------------------

5.24   Non-standard units

Length provides a special case here, since the most convenient (and traditional) units are associated with parts of the body – feet, paces, spans, etc.

Body units

Body units vary from person to person, but the same person can use his or her pace or reach, for example, in different places and at different times, confident that they will remain approximately the same.

CLASS ACTIVITY

Spanning and pacing

Divide the class into groups. Assign each group a rectangular object, such as a table top or a notice board, for measuring with hand-spans, and two straight distances on the ground, such as the length and breadth of the classroom, to measure using paces. Each group should keep a record of all their results in a table, listing the names in the group:

Name	Object: *Table Top* Length (hand-spans)	Breadth	Distances between posts A to B (paces)	B to C
David	8	5	12	15
Vincent	$7\frac{1}{2}$	5	13	17
Mary	10	6	15	20
Ben	10	7	16	21

Note. Hand-spans should be stretched comfortably, not over-stretched or pressed down on the surface. Paces are measured heel-to-heel: they should be comfortable walking paces and not over-stretched.

———————————— ◆ ————————————

Ask the children, 'Were your spans too long? Did you need to use 'bits' (halves, etc.)?'

Discuss each group's results with them. Are they consistent? For example, if A's length was many more spans than B's, was that true also of his breadth? (If not, maybe somebody should check again.)

Is the length twice the breadth?

Children should copy and complete sentences such as:

Mary and Ben found the same number of spans for the length of the table.

David used more spans than Vincent because his span is shorter than Vincent's.

David took 3 paces fewer than I did.

Arbitrary units

Arbitrary units use convenient available objects, e.g. biro pens, exercise book lengths, paper clips. To start with, children need to lay out a whole line of these objects filling the length to be measured. Later, they can use just two of the unit objects, moving one in front of the other in turn.

Small groups of children should all measure the same lengths and compare their results, e.g.

Use counting sticks (all approximately the same length) for the length and height or width of the blackboard.

Use sheets of newspaper for the length and breadth of the classroom.

Discuss the following points with the class:

Which unit would be most suitable for a particular task? (Paper clips are too short for the length of a room.)

How do you manage with 'bits'? Can you estimate halves/quarters? Could you use a second, smaller unit? If so, how are the units related? (A counting stick might be about 6 paper clips; the length of a table might be 8 sticks 2 paper clips.)

Can you round a measurement *to the nearest* unit? (More than $3\frac{1}{2}$ sticks is '4 sticks, to the nearest stick'.)

Wherever possible, compare different lengths:

'The length of the blackboard is more than the height of the door'.

Comparison can be quantified *by difference*:

'The length is four paper clips more than the width'.

Comparison *by ratio* is a later development, but very important:

'The distance to the flagpole is about five times the length of the classroom'.

Estimation

Until children have experience of measuring with a unit, there is no point in their trying to estimate; estimation is only possible and worthwhile when related to known quantities. Encourage children who have this experience and knowledge to estimate before making a new measurement. An estimate must not be just a guess. For example,

A boy paces the length of a room; its length is 12 paces. He looks at the width and estimates it as 8 paces. He then paces the width, and checks his estimate.

A girl measures the cover of her exercise book using match sticks. She then estimates the length and breadth of her text book – how many more, or fewer, match sticks than the exercise book?

5.25   Standard (metric) units of length

To start with, we use the *metre* (m) and the *centimetre* (cm). Later on children will use *millimetres* (mm) and will learn about the *kilometre* (km). A standard metre rule should be kept in the classroom for children to refer to and use. An accurate metre strip can be made from sheets of newspaper by placing one over the other to give the correct length. Tear them together as shown in Fig. 5.2 to hold them in place.

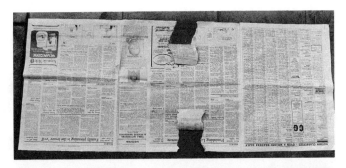

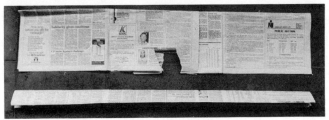

Fig. 5.2

Metre activities

Using the strip, children can:

a) Measure the classroom length and breadth in metres.

b) Measure the door height (usually 2 m) and width (about $\frac{3}{4}$ m).

c) Make a list of several lengths which are a bit more than one metre (say, up to $1\frac{1}{2}$ m).

d) Make a list of several lengths less than 1 m but more than $\frac{3}{4}$ m.

e) Measure their own height (about $1\frac{1}{2}$ m) and waist (less than 1 m!).

f) Measure the circumference of a cylindrical water tank. A metre rule is not convenient for distances of more than a few metres. For these, some form of tape measure is useful – pupils can work together to make one, provided that they have a 'standard' metre to refer to. A length of string, cut to about $5\frac{1}{4}$ m, can be marked in metres by tying small knots at one metre intervals. Small twigs can be put in the knots. Fold each metre in half and mark the $\frac{1}{2}$ m intervals with felt tip pen.

g) Find outdoor distances, e.g. between classroom doors, or round a circular flowerbed, to the nearest $\frac{1}{2}$ m.

h) Mark out a track at 5 m intervals up to 20 m or further. Find how many paces each pupil takes to walk 20 m and, hence, 100 m, 1 km, etc. Each pupil can then try, by counting paces, to walk 10 m or 20 m in some other place.

Measuring in metres and centimetres

A metre is divided into 100 centimetres (cm), but, to start with, we can simply use 10 cm and 5 cm intervals.

When the metre strip (see Fig. 5.2) has been labelled every 10 cm children can measure distances less than a metre quite accurately to the nearest 10 cm, or even 5 cm. (They can imagine 5 cm divisions midway between the 10 cm ones.)

Activities (a)–(f) above can now be repeated, measuring to the nearest 10 cm or 5 cm and, in some cases, even interpolated to the nearest centimetre.

Using the walking track (h) and a marked metre strip, each pupil can walk ten paces and measure the distance to the nearest 10 cm. This will then give his or her *average pace length to the nearest centimetre*! Record this in the pupil's exercise book.

The 30 cm rule

Children may have a ruler bought from a shop, but can also make a flexible rule from a sheet of A4 paper when folded as shown in Fig. 5.3. *Note.* The length of A4 is 297 mm, close enough to 30 cm for practical classroom work.

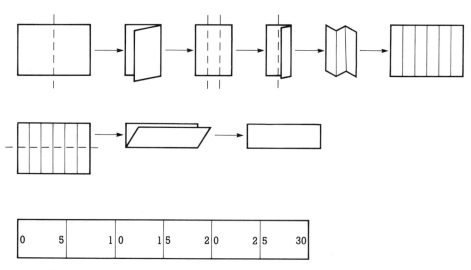

Fig. 5.3

They can use it to measure straight and curved lengths, and learn to *interpolate* between the 5 cm marks. With practice they can measure to the nearest centimetre, e.g. the width of an A4 sheet is 21 cm. Note that this ruler has zero at the end (unlike most rulers sold in shops, which have a 'dead' section outside each end of the scale), so it is easier for beginners to use without error.

A group of pupils can make a table of some of their body measurements in cm:

Name	Handspan	Foot length	Wrist	Ankle
Charles	16 cm	23 cm	15 cm	20 cm

Some of these can be displayed and labelled on a wallchart, made by the children themselves. For example, they can draw round one another's hands and feet, cut round the outlines and glue them to a piece of display card.

Metres and centimetres – recording

A child walks ten paces, and measures the distance walked as 6 m 20 cm. This is (600 + 20) cm, i.e. 620 cm; the average pace length is therefore 62 cm. It is important to be able to change from metres and centimetres into centimetres alone. With such metric units this is straightforward. A child's height may be 1 m 53 cm, or 153 cm or 1.53 m. Once some work on decimals has been done, using two decimal places, the last of these can be used to encourage the understanding of decimals. In fact, we prefer 153 cm or 1.53 m to the use of *two* units (1 m 53 cm) once pupils understand decimal notation. At a later stage pupils need to measure to the nearest millimetre and should record lengths *either* in millimetres (74 mm) *or* in centimetres (7.4 cm). Similarly, distances between villages should be given in kilometres using decimal notation, e.g. 3.8 km. This is how the odometer (distance recorder) of a vehicle shows the distance travelled.

With metric units, it is preferable to *record quantities using one unit only*, but children must first have a clear understanding of the relationships between units and the meaning of decimal notation.

Estimation

Children can try to estimate the heights of their friends and of their teacher. (If the teacher can walk through the door, then he must be less than 2 m tall!) If pupils have marked out a 20 m track then they should try to estimate the distance from, say, their classroom to the school office. They can then check this by pacing having discovered their pace length. They can also see how accurate they can be with other body measurements. For example, knowing the length of their handspan they can span a table length to give an approximation in centimetres, which they can then check by using rule or tape.

5.26   Accurate measurement

Remember that *measurement is always approximate*, even when it is most precise. In engineering, for example, a component may be manufactured within a *tolerance* of 0.01 mm : this means that its length will be within this amount of its stated measurement. By everyday standards this is extremely accurate. Using ordinary equipment we cannot measure more accurately than to the nearest millimetre assuming that our ruler or tape measure itself has been manufactured accurately.

We measure our heights to the nearest centimetre. If your height is given as 172 cm, then this means that, when measured, it was between 171.5 cm and 172.5 cm. You would not give the distance between two towns about 20 km apart, to the nearest metre, or even 100 m, because the towns themselves may be more than a kilometre across ; a sensible measurement would state the distance to the nearest kilometre.

The intelligent measurer should know roughly how accurate are his or her measurements.

5.27   Problem solving

Questions which arise in a practical situation and which involve computation with the units of measurement should always be realistic. Ideally, in the classroom, they should arise from a piece of practical measurement. Most of the following examples are left without actual measurements given, to encourage the students to make some themselves and so work out the answers to the questions.

Practical activities

1   Measure the height of a pile of ten identical exercise books. What is the thickness of one book ?

2 What is the thickness of a sheet of paper? (Use a packet or pad of sheets.)

3 How many sheets of newspaper would you need to cover the floor of your classroom?

4 How many cars could be parked conveniently at right angles to the wall of a building? (Allow sufficient room for the drivers to get out!)

5 How could you measure the diameter of a flagpole or post?

6 Working with a partner, measure and record your 'vital statistics'. For each measurement, consider how accurate your recorded result is.

7 Find a method for measuring the diameter of a long piece of cotton thread.

5.3 MASS

Unfortunately, the terms 'mass' and 'weight' have become confused in everyday English. The *mass* of a body can be defined as the *amount of matter* which it contains. Any body which has a mass on the Earth also has a *weight*, owing to the gravitational pull of the Earth. Mass is measured in grams (g), kilograms (kg), tonnes (t), etc.

Weight is a force – the force with which an object is attracted by the Earth (or the moon, if it is taken there) – and this changes depending on where the object is. A body will weigh more by the sea shore than at the top of Mount Kilimanjaro; it will weigh even less in a jumbo jet flying at 10 000 metres above sea level, and nothing at all if it is taken in a spacecraft beyond the Earth's gravitational pull. But its *mass never changes*. Force is measured in newtons, and a body with a mass of one kilogram has a weight at sea level of about ten newtons.

However, when we use a balance with two scale pans we are able to compare the masses on each pan because the heavier mass is more strongly attracted by the Earth, i.e. it has the greater weight. We talk of weighing things, but we must remember that the quantity measured is their *mass*.

Some kind of balance is an essential piece of classroom equipment. Ideally there should be several, so that each group of, say, six pupils can use one. If this is not possible, the teacher should plan for one group to use the balance while others are doing different work – this is often the best solution when equipment is scarce, and needs careful planning over several lessons. The balance described below uses junk material which is readily available in many places. It can actually give better results than more ambitious ones made from pieces of wood.

FOR THE TEACHER TO MAKE

A light-duty balance

This costs very little to make, and will weigh objects up to about 150 grams to the nearest gram. (For weighing heavier objects, another design is described on p. 114.)

Materials required

A plastic bottle, capacity 750 ml – 1 l and 25–30 cm in height. (Most bottles of washing-up liquid, bleach, toilet cleanser, or $\frac{1}{2}$ l engine oil bottles, etc., thoroughly cleaned, are suitable.)
A plain wooden 30 cm ruler
4 paper clips
2 milk cartons, or the bases of 2 more plastic containers
String (or at least 6 more paper clips)
A nail, or other sharp instrument, for boring holes.

1 Make a hole in the middle of the ruler, fairly close to one edge. Make two more holes to hold the paper clips, at an equal distance from each end of the ruler and close to the other long edge.

2 Open the middle bend in three of the paper clips; then insert one through each of the holes in the ruler (see Fig. 5.4).

3 Cut slots measuring about 8 cm by 1 cm in opposite sides of the bottle, using a blade or sharp scissors. Insert small stones, or sand, through these holes to stabilise the base.

4 Make two holes through the neck of the bottle, and insert a straightened paper clip through them to form a bridge across the neck; depress the bridge a little, so that the ruler can hang on it. Pass the ruler through the slots in the bottle and hook the centre paper clip over the bridge.

5 Make two scale pans using the cartons or cut-down plastic containers, and hang them from the ends of the ruler using string or more paper clips as shown in Fig. 5.4.

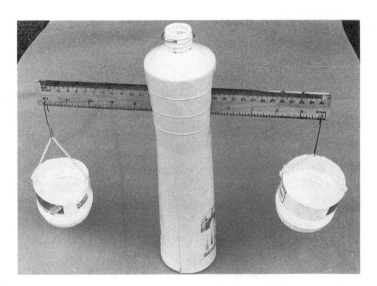

Fig. 5.4

Note. The ruler can be adjusted so that it is horizontal by trimming small pieces off one of the scale pans.

———————— ◆ ————————

5.31 Vocabulary

Children should pick up *heavy* and *light* objects for comparison. For example, the teacher might have in the classroom two stones, one large and heavy, one small and light, and a 5-litre jerrycan. The large stone is heavy, the empty jerrycan is light (by comparison) but the full jerrycan is heavier than the stone.

To compare objects, we *weigh* them on a balance. The heavy object 'goes down', the light object 'goes up'.

5.32 Conservation of mass

Start with two lumps of clay, moulded to look the same ; check with the balance that their masses are the same. Mould one lump into a completely different form. Ask the children which piece of clay now weighs more. Now break one lump into several smaller ones. Ask the children, 'Can I balance the big lump with the smaller ones ? Do I need to use them all ? Do I need more than I have got ?'

5.33   Comparison

Comparing two masses
First, children should try, by lifting, to judge which of two similar objects is *the heavier*. They can then try to compare objects which are unlike one another in shape or size, e.g. stone and a book. Pupils should check their 'feeling' estimates with the balance.

Comparing and ordering three or more masses
Again, estimates by lifting can be followed by the use of the balance. Objects which look similar can be used first, then use contrasting objects.

CLASS ACTIVITY

Comparing masses

Using objects which look alike but have different masses

For the teacher to prepare
Fill five identical containers with two different masses of, e.g. sand, soil, stones, rice, beans, etc. The space above the main filling material can be filled with screwed-up pieces of paper, to prevent rattling (which could affect your judgement later).

The pupil activity
1 Pick each container up and, by 'feel', decide which is the heaviest and which the lightest.

2 Try to arrange all five in order, from heaviest to lightest.

3 Check the order by using a balance.

Note. A set of smooth stones, of various shapes and sizes, could be used instead of containers. Letters can be scratched or marked with a pen on them.

Using contrasted objects
These must still be small enough to fit easily in the scale pans. They could include, for example, a pen, an eraser, sheet of paper (screwed up), a bean and a bottle top.

———————◆———————

5.34 Non-standard units and estimation

You need a plentiful supply of fairly small objects which can be used as units. Bottle caps (from beer or mineral/soda bottles), nails, small low-value coins, are suitable.

Using the balance, pupils should weigh some of the objects used for ordering in Section 5.33. They should always record their results, e.g. in tabular form:

	Balances with	
Object	Nails	Bottle Tops

Check that the two sets of results give the same order for the objects. Are they roughly proportional? (Is the ratio of nails to bottle tops roughly the same for each object?) Very light objects will require a smaller unit, such as match sticks or dried beans.

When pupils have weighed one or two objects using the same unit they can estimate the masses of others. Results can be tabulated:

	Mass (bottle tops)	
Container	Estimate	Measured
C		25
A	30	33
E	45	

5.35 Standard units

For classroom use the kilogram is, in general, too large. But the gram is so small that weighing may involve hundreds of grams, so a 'basic' mass for practical use needs to be somewhere in between. Most convenient would be a 10 g mass, so it is worth trying to find some way of making 10 g fairly simply and at low cost.

(Low denomination coins may be appropriate to use; it is quite easy to fasten a stack of these together, using sticky tape, to make a 100 g mass.) Standard bottle caps weigh about $2\frac{1}{2}$ g, and can be fastened in fours to make 10 g masses.

Heavier units, e.g. 500 g ($\frac{1}{2}$ kg) can be made by using suitable bottles or jars and filling them with water to a certain depth.

For weighing larger masses a more substantial balance is needed. A fairly simple one can, again, be made using a wooden school ruler and some pieces of junk.

FOR THE TEACHER TO MAKE

A heavy-duty balance

This balance will weigh masses up to one kilogram, to an accuracy of ten grams.

Materials required

A tin lid, about 10 cm diameter

A piece of wood, approximately 2 cm × 5 cm × 10 cm

A nail of length 3–4 cm, preferably with a large flat head

2 smaller nails

Ruler, paper clips, string and milk cartons as for the light-duty balance described on p. 110.

1 Make holes in the ruler as for the light-duty balance.

2 Fasten the wooden block to the tin lid with the two smaller nails, so that the lid extends beyond the wood by between 5 mm and 10 mm.

3 Nail the ruler, through the centre hole, to the wood at a point about 2 cm above the tin lid, so that the ruler will swing freely, without excessive play. (The ruler should be restrained by the lid, when it is inclined at a small angle.)

4 Fasten scale pans to hang from the end holes in the ruler. Fold down the rims of the cartons to give them the strength to support masses up to 1 kg (see Fig. 5.5).

Fig. 5.5

If there is a local hospital or dispensary nearby, there may be a suitable balance or set of scales for weighing patients; it might be possible to arrange for children to use this, either at school or wherever it is normally kept, to find their own masses. It is difficult to give children practical experience of *kilograms* unless a manufactured balance is available.

Relating units, and recording

Because 1 kg = 1000 g, to write a quantity given in grams as kilograms requires three decimal places: 625 g = 0.625 kg. It is important to know that 10 g is 0.01 kg, and 100 g is 0.1 kg. (These units are the *dekagram* (dag) and the *hectogram* (hg); however, these names are not in common use, and it is better if children know them as ten and hundred gram units, and that a kilo is a thousand grams.)

Collect some printed food packets and discuss the quantities stated '100 g net', '350 g', 'min 70 g' – how accurately have the quantities been measured?

For very heavy objects the standard unit is the *tonne* (1 t = 1000 kg). A small car has a mass of less than 1 t, a Landrover more than 2 t. Pupils could try to find out the *tare weight*, i.e. the mass when unloaded, of larger vehicles. This information is often marked on the chassis. Masses can be given either in tonnes or in kilograms, e.g. 2250 kg = 2.25 t.

Estimation

Standard food packages can be shown to pupils, e.g. a 2 kg bag of flour or rice; they can lift it, and then estimate how many long-life (UHT) milk packets would be needed to balance it. (A $\frac{1}{2}$ l packet weighs almost exactly $\frac{1}{2}$ kg.)

5.36   Accurate weighing

In the primary school it is very unlikely that there will be equipment for really precise measurement of mass, e.g. to an accuracy closer than 10 g or 5 g.

Labels on medicines may show quantities in milligrams (1 g = 1000 mg). Pupils should realise that masses on packets and bottles may only be accurate to within 5 per cent. You would expect to give your own mass to the nearest kilogram.

5.37   Problem solving

Many of the following problems require the student to obtain data either by weighing or by referring to masses printed on objects, or using reference material. The solver should ask,

'What data am I given?'
'What further data do I need?'
'How do I then process the data?'
'What arithmetical operations must I carry out, and in what order?'
'What degree of accuracy is needed?'
'How should I give the answer?'

1 Find the mass of one paper clip.

2 Using an unopened, labelled packet of A4 paper, calculate its mass
   from the data on the label. Check by weighing.

3 In a lift there is a notice saying 'Maximum load 1200 kg'. How many
   adults could safely ride in this lift?

4 Several pupils should each count out 100 grains of rice, or beans. Put
   all the rice together in a container and weigh it. How many grains
   would you find in a kilogram?

5 At a social function tea is served, and on average two teaspoons of
   sugar are taken with each cup of tea. How many people can be served
   from a kilo of sugar?

6 A wooden crate contains 24 bottles each containing 300 ml of drink.
   What is the difference in its mass when the bottles are all empty?
   Given that the crate of full bottles weighs 18 kg, estimate the mass of
   an empty bottle.

5.4 CAPACITY

The concepts of *capacity* and *volume* are closely related; volume is
generally associated with solid objects, and capacity with quantities of
fluid.

   One litre (l) is the capacity of a *decimetre cube* (10 cm × 10 cm ×
10 cm) so 1000 millilitres (ml) is equivalent to 1000 cubic centimetres
(cc). In this way the metric units of capacity and volume are closely
linked. Children should first compare the capacities of containers by
filling them with sand, water, or other substances which can be poured.
Volume is best introduced by building solid shapes with unit blocks, e.g.
match boxes or (ideally) 1 cm or 2 cm cubes.

5.41 Vocabulary

Using several cups, jars or small tins of various capacities, pour from one
container to another. Ask pupils, 'Which one *holds more*?', 'Does this
one *fill* that one?', and observe, for example, 'That one *holds too much* to
go into the cup', or 'These two *hold about the same amount*'.

5.42 Conservation of capacity (or volume)

You need several (three or four) jars or bottles made of glass or clear plastic, a funnel to pour through, and a suitable unit container such as a cup, or a small tin. The jars and bottles should have different diameters, so that equal quantities of fluid will reach different levels in them.

Pour equal amounts into different jars while the children are watching then ask, 'Which one has more in it?'

Pour from one container into another and ask, 'Has the amount of water/sand changed? Is there more now, or less?'

5.43 Direct comparison of capacities

Comparing two containers

Containers which have different shapes or proportions cannot be compared 'by eye' – appearances are deceptive.

Children should be given, to start with, simple common objects – empty tins, cups, cartons – and compare their capacities by pouring dry sand, or water, from one into the other.

Ordering several small containers

Choose four different containers which you think will hold roughly the same amount, between, for example, 200 ml and 300 ml.

Estimate, by looking, which you think to be the largest, which next, and so on, arranging them in order.

Check your order in each of the following ways:

1 By filling them, with water or sand, and tipping the contents from one container into another

2 By filling each container in turn and tipping its contents into a much larger container, marking the level which each one reaches on the large container.

Record your results as shown below.

1	Two containers compared	Larger/Smaller
	A and C	C larger than A
	B and C	C larger than B

2 Order of size of containers (largest first)

C	B	A	D

5.44 Non-standard units and estimation

Compare the same containers used in Section 5.43 by filling each one with a *unit* container, smaller than any of those to be measured. Suitable units might be a film box or a large spoon.

As with the comparison of masses (see Section 5.34) pupils should try to estimate the capacity of the next container before measuring it.

CLASS ACTIVITY

Calibrating a measuring jar

Each group of pupils needs a straight-sided jar, such as a jam jar. Glue a strip of paper down the outside, or fasten it at the top and bottom with small pieces of sticky tape. Fill the unit container and pour its contents into the jar; mark the level of the water or sand. (Better results are obtained with water which immediately forms a level surface ; sand and other dry fillings need to settle, and do not give a perfectly level surface.)

Repeat this, marking each unit level on the paper. In this way they have *calibrated* the jar by marking a scale of units as in Fig. 5.6.

Fig. 5.6

Are the unit divisions equally spaced? (If the unit is very small it is better to mark the level every 5 or 10 units, and then to rely on interpolation.)

Pupils can now check the capacities of other containers by pouring their contents into the calibrated jar.

———————— ◆ ————————

5.45   Standard units

Litres and *millilitres* are the only units of capacity in common use although manufacturers will sometimes give a capacity in *decilitres* (1 dl = 100 ml = 0.1 l) or *centilitres* (1 cl = 10 ml = 0.01 l). For example, a standard wine bottle contains 70 cl. In general, it is better to use millilitres only for quantities less than a litre. As with masses measured in grams, this means that pupils are dealing with tens and hundreds of units from an early stage.

5.46   Accurate measurement of capacity

The first need is a unit which can be used to calibrate other containers. Take a full mineral or beer bottle which is marked as containing 300 ml, and then find three more empty identical bottles. Fill one of the empty bottles to the same level as the full one. Then divide its contents, using a funnel to prevent spillage, equally between the empty bottles, so that each then contains 100 ml. This may not be perfectly accurate (manufacturers usually fill containers with *more* than the stated contents), but will serve as a reasonable standard.

FOR THE TEACHER TO MAKE

A measuring cylinder

Choose a jar made of glass or clear plastic, or a plastic bottle whose top can be cut off. The main body must be a true cylinder, constant in diameter. Nearly all such jars have a base which is not cylindrical: this part cannot be used for measuring.

1   Using a standard decilitre (see above), mark levels on the jar at 100 ml, 200 ml, 300 ml, ... You should find that these 100 ml divisions are equally spaced.

2   Using a ruler, divide these 100 ml divisions each into 5 or 10 equal subdivisions. Label every 50 ml or 100 ml.

3 Copy the positions of these 100 ml divisions onto a narrow strip of paper.

4 Fix the strip of paper onto the cylinder in the correct position with sticky tape as in Fig. 5.7.

Fig. 5.7

———————————— ♦ ————————————

Such a measuring cylinder will prove to be a valuable aid when doing practical work on volume (see Chapter 7). Meanwhile, pupils can use it to find the capacity of various small common objects, e.g.

A drinking glass or cup (usually 200 ml – 250 ml)
A standard dessert spoon (10 ml)
A teaspoon (less than 5 ml),

as well as other containers chosen by the teacher. For the smaller ones, fill and pour them several times into the measuring cylinder; for example, twenty spoonfuls might give a scale reading of say, 180 ml, an average of 9 ml.

To fill any narrow-necked container it is helpful to have some form of funnel. This can be done quite easily using paper (for dry fillings, such as sand) or liquid-proof card, such as from milk cartons, and some sticky tape. Alternatively, the top of a plastic bottle can be cut off and used as a funnel.

Larger capacities – litres

Most classroom activity will concern capacities less than, or not much more than, one litre, but pupils should have a rough idea of the capacities of other common objects, e.g.

A bucket,

A jerrycan,

A bowl for washing clothes or dishes.

Provided that there is no water shortage, a class can discover these capacities. Given a litre, or half-litre, container, they can fill a bucket or bowl. Plastic jerrycans usually hold 5 l, 10 l, and 20 l ; if the capacity of a small one is known, pupils can estimate, and then check, the capacity of larger ones.

A class could also be asked to find out the fuel capacity of certain vehicles, by observation at a local filling station. If a school has a water storage tank, pupils should know its capacity.

5.47   Problem solving

As with length and mass (Sections 5.27 and 5.37) students should obtain suitable data for themselves where it is not included in the following examples.

1   How many jerrycans full of water will be needed to provide 100 cups of tea ?

2   Find out how many $\frac{1}{2}$ litre packets of milk will be needed for 100 cups of tea.

3   A car uses 7 litres while travelling 100 km. How many full tanks will it use on a round trip ?

4   Estimate the amount of water used by a student each day,

   a)   for drinking

   b)   for washing.

For how many days would a 500 litre storage tank meet the needs of a dormitory of 40 students ?

CHAPTER SIX

Shapes and Angles

6.1 INTRODUCTION

In their early years, children should learn to identify and name different shapes, both plane and solid. Later they will learn more formal relationships between shapes, distances and directions – the study of geometry. The word *geometry* comes from the ancient Greek language and means Earth measurement (*geo-metria*).

6.11 Vocabulary

In two dimensions we look at the sizes of *sides* and *angles*; in three dimensions we look at the *faces* of a solid – are they *plane* or *curved*? – and at the shapes of the faces made by the *edges* which form their boundaries. In this study, children have to develop a large vocabulary of words, many of them special to geometry, e.g.

parallel opposite congruent
perpendicular adjacent similar.

Teachers and pupils must use these words precisely to avoid confusion. For example,

the *side* of a triangle, but the triangular *face* of a prism, bounded by *edges*, a *segment* of a circle, bounded by a *chord* and an *arc*.

6.12 Plane shapes

Many common plane shapes are special cases of more general shapes. For example,

a *square* is a special kind of *rectangle*,
a *rectangle* is a special kind of *parallelogram*,
a *parallelogram* is a *quadrilateral* with its opposite sides parallel.

Teaching should begin with these special shapes, and in their early study, the concept of *symmetry* helps to bring together what might otherwise seem to be a collection of isolated facts.

6.2 SYMMETRY

6.21 Line symmetry

The most obvious kind of symmetry is *mirror* or *line* symmetry when the two halves of a shape or design mirror each other in a straight line, the *axis* or *line of symmetry*. Children can make 'devils' by putting a blob of wet ink or paint on a sheet of paper then folding it with a firm crease and pressing the folded halves together. The crease is the axis of symmetry.

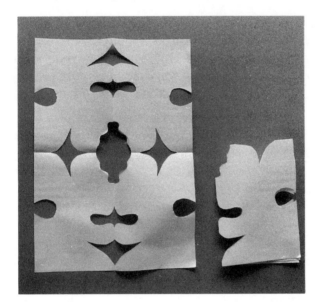

Fig. 6.1

Fig. 6.1 shows a sheet which has been folded into four (with two folds), cut, and then opened out: the result is a pattern with two axes of symmetry (the fold lines) which are at right angles to each other. Folding and cutting in this way teaches young children about symmetry, and gives opportunities for creativity and enjoyment.

6.22 Rotational symmetry

The shapes in Fig. 6.2 (overleaf) show another kind of symmetry: each can be turned round or *rotated*, so that it looks the same in new positions.

The best known examples of this are the capital letters N, S and Z which can be turned upside down but still look the same; they have *half-turn symmetry*. The logos in Fig. 6.2 have $\frac{1}{4}$-turn and $\frac{1}{3}$-turn symmetry respectively. Notice that neither of these examples has any line of symmetry.

Fig. 6.2

Look at the opened sheet in Fig. 6.1 – it has half-turn symmetry, as well as the two axes of symmetry. Fig. 6.3 shows some of the commonest shapes which children study in the classroom. You should be able to name them and, in each case, say whether the shape has one or more axes of symmetry, and whether it has rotational symmetry.

Fig. 6.3

6.3 INTRODUCING ANGLES

The development of the concept of *angle* begins with pupils identifying *right angles*, and later contrasting them with other angles (known as *acute, obtuse, reflex*). Two aspects of angle are important – the amount of *turning* or *rotation* from one direction to another, and the angle *shape* formed by these two direction lines – the *arms* of the angle. The rotation aspect is very important later when pupils learn to measure angles with a protractor.

The right angle is a very common shape, seen at the corners of walls, books, tables, and so on. The *quarter turn* is the rotation which makes a right angle, and it is familiar from the quarter-hour turns of the minute hand on a clock.

CLASS ACTIVITY

Quarter-turns

This activity is most easily done out of doors. Pupils should work in groups of four. Each pupil needs a long, straight pointer; this could be a stick (a length of bamboo, for example) or a tightly rolled page of a newspaper, fastened with sticky tape or a staple.

1   One pupil lays a pointer on the ground, faces in that direction, and turns with his eyes closed.

2   Make a quarter-turn; a second pupil lays his pointer in the direction the turner is facing.

3   The turner makes a second quarter-turn (i.e. a half-turn altogether), and a third member of the group lays his pointer in the direction faced.

4   Make one more quarter turn, and the fourth member's pointer is laid on the ground.

5   The group looks at the pattern of the four pointers. *Do the pointers make a cross of four equal quarter turns?*

Note that the pairs of opposite pointers should form straight lines: two right angles make a straight angle.

---◆---

In doing the activity above, children learn to link the quarter-turn with the right-angle shape. This can be made very easily by the well-known paper folding method shown in Fig. 6.4.

Fig. 6.4

Pupils can quickly learn to identify right angles, and can be given a worksheet on which they have to mark the right angles. Make a set of cut-out angles from thick card, for the children to handle themselves. About half the angles should be accurate right angles, about a quarter should be slightly acute, and the rest slightly obtuse. This will make the pupils consider carefully which angles are right angles. (Children must understand that the *angle size* does not depend on the *length of the arms*. Make sure that some of the smaller angles have long arms, and some of the obtuse angles have quite short arms.) If there are at least four cut-out right angles, children can place them together to show the cross of perpendicular lines. Other angles can be compared by laying them on top of one another, leading to the ideas of *acute* and *obtuse*.

6.4 POLYGONS

A plane figure with straight sides is called a *polygon*. The sides of a polygon meet at *vertices*; at each vertex the two sides form an angle. A polygon which has all sides equal in length, and all angles at the vertices equal, is called *regular*.

A *square* is a regular *quadrilateral* (a 4-sided polygon). Any regular polygon has two kinds of symmetry. Fig. 6.5 shows a regular pentagon has five axes of symmetry (shown as broken lines) and also has rotational symmetry – a rotation of $\frac{1}{5}$ of a full turn about the centre will bring the next vertex to the top of the diagram, so that it looks the same.

Fig. 6.5

A *convex* polygon has all its angles less than a straight angle; when drawn on a piece of card and cut out, a convex polygon can be rolled along a table, and all its sides and vertices in turn will touch the table. But a *concave* polygon 'caves in' at some vertices (see Fig. 6.6): some of its angles are *reflex* – *more* than a straight angle.

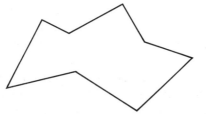

Fig. 6.6

6.41   Triangles
Triangles can have many different shapes, depending on the sizes of the three angles. Pupils should learn to identify triangles as being either
> *right-angled* (i.e. one right angle)

or *obtuse-angled* (i.e. one obtuse angle)
or *acute-angled* (i.e. all three angles acute).
> They should also learn that

> a triangle with all sides equal is *equilateral*
> a triangle with two equal sides is *isosceles*
> a triangle with three unequal sides is *scalene*.

Teachers should make a set of different kinds of triangle, made from thick card, which children can handle and study carefully.

6.42   Cutting and folding activities
Pupils can learn about many shapes and their properties through simple paper-folding and cutting, or tearing. The following activities introduce many shape names and descriptive words. For these, use sheets of paper which are half-blank, i.e. have been used on one side. Preferably, use the popular A4 size, which is shorter and wider than foolscap.

Making a trapezium
Take a sheet of paper, and fold it corner to opposite corner (see Fig. 6.7a). Crease the fold firmly, and then tear carefully along it (a ruler edge is helpful here). The two pieces are exactly the same, or *congruent* (see Fig. 6.7b). The shape is a *trapezium* – two of its sides are *parallel*. Two of the angles are right-angles, one is acute, and the other obtuse.

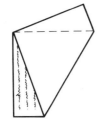
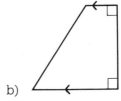

Fig. 6.7   a)   b)

Check that the four sides of each trapezium are unequal in length by holding the sides of one against those of the other.

Make new shapes, using both pieces and placing them so that one pair of equal sides is together, as in Fig. 6.8a.

There are eight shapes altogether, including the original rectangle. Note that, if one piece shows its blank face and the other its used face, then the combined shape has a line of symmetry.

The shapes made in this way are shown in Fig. 6.8b – an *isosceles trapezium*, two *pentagons* (one convex, one concave) – and Fig. 6.8a, a concave *hexagon*.

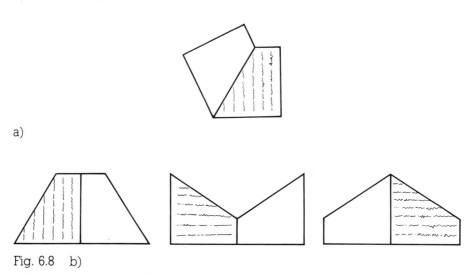

a)

Fig. 6.8   b)

If the pieces are placed with both blank faces showing, then we can make the original rectangle, and also a *parallelogram* and two hexagons, one of them concave. All of these, seen in Fig. 6.9, have half-turn symmetry.

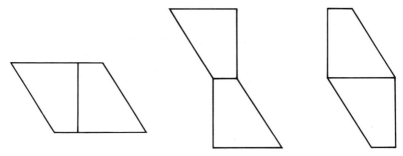

Fig. 6.9

Making a rhombus

Fold a sheet corner to opposite corner. Crease the fold firmly, and look at the outline of the folded sheet (see Fig. 6.10a). The shape is a pentagon. It has one axis of symmetry, and two of its angles are right angles.

Fold the pentagon along the line of symmetry and, again, look at the folded shape (see Fig. 6.10b). This is a quadrilateral, with four unequal sides. Two of its opposite angles are right angles.

Next, fold the outer triangles over the inner ones, along the edge of the sheet (see Fig. 6.10c). Now open the sheet and look at the shapes made by the fold lines seen in Fig. 6.10d.

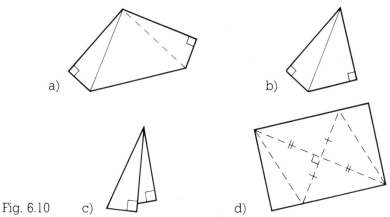

Fig. 6.10

There are six right-angled triangles. Four of them are congruent (the middle ones), and the other two are also congruent, but smaller than the four. The four large triangles make a *rhombus* – a parallelogram with four equal sides.

Note that the diagonals of the rhombus (the first two fold lines) bisect each other at right-angles – they are the axes of symmetry of the rhombus.

Making a square

Fold a sheet side to *adjacent* side to form an isosceles right-angled triangle (see Fig. 6.11).

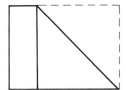

Fig. 6.11

Then crease and tear off the rectangular strip on the left, leaving a *square*. (This is the easiest way to make a square.)

Making a regular pentagon

Give each pair of pupils a sheet of newspaper measuring about 60 cm by 40 cm. Tear this carefully in half, so that each has a piece about 60 cm by 20 cm. Each pupil must fold his piece to make a strip, three layers thick which has parallel sides ; use the lines of type on the paper to help here. When folded, the strip should be about 6–7 cm wide, and still 60 cm long. Loop the strip over, and make a simple knot, easing the strip carefully into the knot before pressing it flat. Tear off the ends of the strip, or fold them behind the knot and tuck the ends inside, leaving just the shape of the knot (see Fig. 6.12).

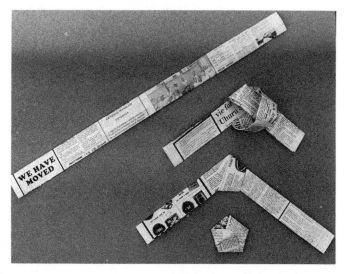

Fig. 6.12

This is a *regular* pentagon. Draw round its outline and then, by turning it round, show that it will fit into the outline with any of the five vertices at the top. The diagonals of the pentagon can be drawn ; one of these should be showing as an edge of the strip. The pattern of the pentagon with its five diagonals, forming a five-pointed star and a smaller 'upside down' pentagon inside, is called a *pentagram* (see Fig. 6.13).

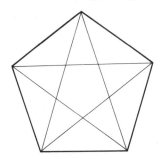

Fig. 6.13

6.5 CIRCLES

6.51 Drawing circles
Most children will eventually learn to draw circles using a pair of compasses, but there is much to be said for first drawing circles with improvised equipment, more readily available. The following suggestions are just a few of many possibilities. Methods (a)–(c) rely on the fact that a circle is the path of a moving point, always the same distance from a fixed point, the centre.

a) Using a strip of card, a pin and a pencil
Pin one end of the card strip to the paper and the table or desk. Make a small hole along the strip, and put the pencil point through it. Hold the paper firmly, and rotate the card strip with the pencil, tracing the circle as the pencil point moves. By making several holes for the pencil point, various sizes of circle can be drawn.

b) Using a pin and a pencil
Pin the paper to the table or desk. Hold the pencil upright with its point on the paper, with one hand. Keep this hand still, and slowly rotate the sheet of paper about the pin. The pencil will trace out a circle.

c) Using a pencil and your hand only!
This time 'pin' the paper to the table with the knuckle of your little finger. At the same time, hold the pencil with its point on the paper, sloping away from the direction in which you are going to rotate the paper. Rotate the paper, and the circle will be drawn.

d) Using any rigid circular object
The simplest method of all is to use a lid, or the rim, of a tin, cooking pan, waste bin or any other rigid object and to draw round it, holding your pencil fairly upright all the way round.

6.52 Finding the centre of a circle
To find the centre of a circular disc of paper, fold it in half along a diameter. A second fold, along a different diameter immediately fixes the centre. If you do not have a disc, but simply a circle drawn on a sheet of paper, you can still fold the circle along a diameter if you hold it up to the light and carefully crease it so that the circle folds on to itself.

CLASS ACTIVITY

Equilateral triangle and regular hexagon

Cut out a paper circle, find the centre, and mark it with a small neat dot. Fold the circle so that the edge or circumference of the disc passes through the centre (see Fig. 6.14a). Crease the fold firmly. Now, make a second fold which starts at one end of the first fold and, again, takes the edge of the disc through the centre as in Fig. 6.14b. A third fold, joining the ends of the first two, should also take the circumference through the centre. The shape of the folded paper is an equilateral triangle.

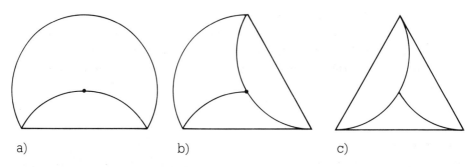

a)   b)   c)

Fig. 6.14

Now fold the triangle along each of its axes of symmetry in turn. (Fold it with the segments already folded inside.) Then open the disc out (see Fig. 6.15). The boundary is a regular hexagon. Note also several smaller equilateral triangles, right-angled and isosceles triangles, and rhombuses.

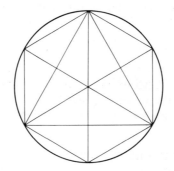

Fig. 6.15

6.53 Tangents to a circle

Draw a circle, and then draw any line. The line may not intersect the circle but, if it does, there will generally be two points of intersection (see Fig. 6.16a). These points are the ends of a *chord* of the circle. If the line just *touches* the circle without crossing the circumference, then the line is a *tangent* to the circle.

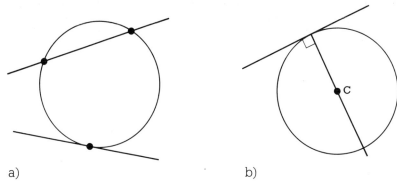

a)   b)

Fig. 6.16

At the point of contact of a tangent to a circle, the line perpendicular to the tangent passes through the centre and is, therefore, a diameter of the circle (see Fig. 6.16b). An everyday example of this is the spoke of a wheel, e.g. a bicycle wheel: the tangent is the level ground and the diameter a pair of spokes.

Practical Point. When drawing a tangent with a ruler to a circle which has already been drawn, place the ruler on the inside edge of the circle.

6.6 SOLID SHAPES

Children begin learning geometry by handling and looking at solids. The commonest geometrical shapes which we use are containers in the form of *cuboids* and *cylinders*, and balls which are *spheres*.

The teacher can show a class two different cartons, e.g. a tall box holding a medicine bottle, and a flat box holding a ream of paper sheets, and ask the children what is the same about them.

The question can also be asked about two different cylinders, e.g. a tin of boot polish and a large tin of cooking fat.

6.61 Polyhedra

Solids with plane faces and straight edges are called *polyhedra* (many faces). A cuboid is an example of a *hexahedron*, with six faces. One important category of polyhedron is the *prism*. A prism has a *uniform cross-section*, the shape of one of its ends. All its other faces are rectangles, and are perpendicular to the two ends. A pencil, if its sharpened end is cut off, is a *hexagonal prism* ; the cross-section is a regular hexagon. Some rulers are also hexagonal prisms, but in this case the section is not a *regular* hexagon. Many simple buildings are *pentagonal prisms* : the end walls show the pentagonal cross-section. Some of these prisms are shown in Fig. 6.17. Although prisms are, in general, polyhedra, we can include cylinders as circular prisms and also cuboids as *rectangular prisms*.

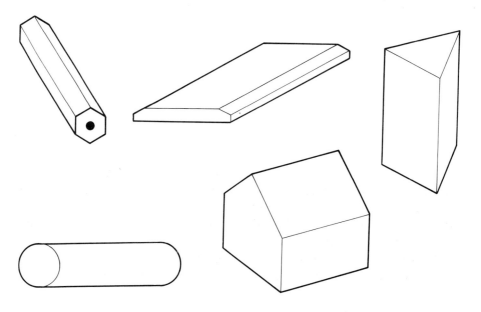

Fig. 6.17

6.62 Horizontal and vertical

Pupils should understand that, in a well-built classroom, the floor is horizontal and the walls are vertical. When a cuboid rests on a horizontal table ask them *which faces are horizontal, which edges are vertical*. The same questions can be asked about prisms such as those shown in Fig. 6.17.

Do not use the blackboard to teach these ideas – the pupils must look carefully at the actual objects. Diagrams copied into exercise books will only confuse, since the blackboard is vertical and the books usually horizontal.

6.63   Nets for polyhedra

Children can learn much, and gain much enjoyment, from making polyhedra from *nets*. The teacher can show, by taking a cuboid such as a soap powder carton, and carefully cutting along some of its edges, how the six rectangular faces are linked and are, in fact, three pairs of congruent rectangles (see Fig. 6.18).

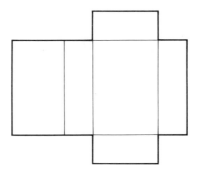

Fig. 6.18

Using ordinary squared exercise book paper, pupils can draw, cut out and fold such nets, learning how to draw them so that the equal sides of the rectangles meet to form edges of the cuboid. A certain amount of inaccuracy must be expected at first, and pupils can learn through their mistakes. When they see edges not meeting correctly they will understand more clearly which ones need to be drawn equal. The special cases of cuboids with *square* ends, or with all six faces square, i.e. *cubes*, should be included in this work.

Other simple solids which can be made from their nets include triangular prisms, square-based pyramids and *tetrahedra* (triangular pyramids).

6.64   Tetrahedron

In some countries the *tetrapak* is commonly used to package milk. This is essentially a tetrahedron, and 18 of these are packed into a crate which is a hexagonal prism.

Such a tetrahedron can be made very simply.

CLASS ACTIVITY

Making a tetrapak

Give pupils a used long envelope (foolscap or 'official' size) measuring about 10 cm by 23 cm, and sealed at the end. Fig. 6.19 shows the stages of making the tetrahedron.

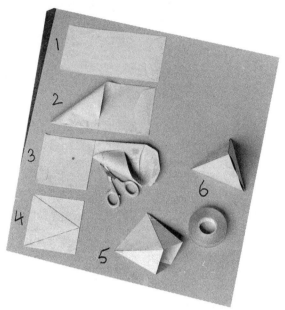

Fig. 6.19

1 Take the end of the envelope which is still sealed, and make a square fold (see Fig. 6.11).

2 Cut off the square end of the envelope, with its sealed end; use this part, and the rest can be thrown away.

3 By folding, find the mid-point of the open end of the square.

4 Join this mid-point to the two opposite corners of the square, using a ruler and pressing hard with a ball-point pen.

5 Fold along these ruled lines and crease the folds firmly.

6 Open the unsealed end, and fasten it with a piece of sticky tape.

The faces are congruent isosceles triangles – *not* equilateral, since the sides of the square are shorter than the fold lines.
Six of these mini tetrapaks can be held together, showing how they will fit inside a regular hexagonal boundary.

6.7 MEASURING ANGLES

The *whole turn* and the *right angle* are the first units of angle measure that children meet. Simple fractions of these can be used in certain special situations. In Fig. 6.20a, the angle between two of the radii is $\frac{1}{7}$ of a whole turn. In Fig. 6.20b the angle between the clock hands is $\frac{2}{3}$ of a right angle. However, it soon becomes clear that we need a smaller unit if we are to compare or measure angles. As with other measures, there is a clear development to be followed as the child masters the concept.

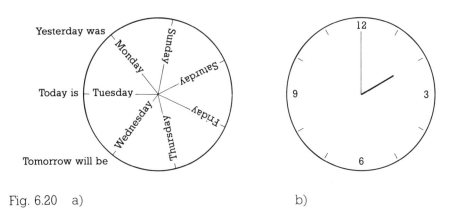

Fig. 6.20   a)   b)

6.71   Comparison

A set of cut-out cardboard angles, similar to those described on p. 126 can be made, and one laid on another for direct comparison. Such a set should contain at least five acute and five obtuse angles ; the lengths of the arms of the angles should be varied, and independent of the angle size. After comparing angles directly in this way, pupils can be asked to arrange angles, drawn on a worksheet, in order of size.

6.72   Arbitrary units

When starting to measure length, children lay out a series of unit sticks, or other *arbitrary* units (see p. 103) to fill the length of the object being measured. In the same way, they need to be given a number of *unit angles* to fill a given angle which they are to measure. The unit described below is fairly simple to make in large quantities and, as we shall see, is also a useful size.

FOR THE TEACHER TO MAKE

Unit angles

1 Divide an A4 sheet of paper into four equal strips (see Fig. 6.21) by careful folding.

2 Draw the diagonals of each strip.

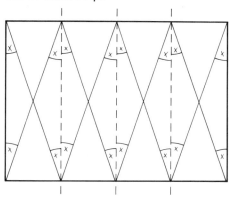

Fig. 6.21

3 Cut out the 16 equal acute angles, so formed (marked x); tear roughly across the ends of the angles so that the outer edge is *not* a straight line; the arms of the angles should be about 10 cm long in each case.

————————————◆————————————

Preparing a worksheet

It happens that the unit angles described above are almost 20°. Prepare a worksheet, therefore, containing angles of the following sizes:

20°   40°   60°   80°   100°   120°   140°   160°

A second worksheet might contain some angles which involve half-units:

30°   50°   70°   90°   etc.

Children must be shown how to lay down the units to 'fill' an angle. They must work from a zero line in a particular direction, or *sense*; it is best if this is always clockwise to start with, because this is the sense of the outer scale of a protractor.

6.73   Degrees – a first protractor

Children should begin by using a protractor with only the 10° intervals marked. Ideally the protractor should be circular, although it is hard to make a serviceable one from card or paper. Fig. 6.22 shows one – the

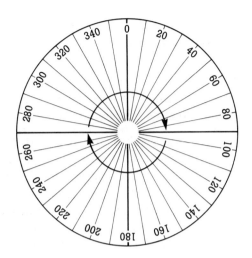

Fig. 6.22

main problem is to make a central hole small enough for pupils to place it on the vertex of the angle accurately enough. A hole punch is needed by the teacher, who probably has to make the whole disc with its rulings.

However, a satisfactory semicircular half disc can be made by each pupil (see Fig. 6.23a) using a card template which the teacher has made and can pass round (see Fig. 6.23b).

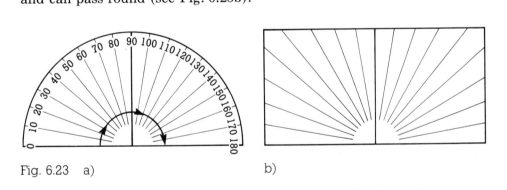

Fig. 6.23   a)   b)

Pupils should draw a circle (using a tin lid, or other means), cut it out and carefully fold it in half. Using the teacher's template the pupil lays his paper semicircle on it with the centre in the correct position, and marks where the 10° lines cross the edge of the paper ; join these marks to the centre. Draw a sense arrow to show that the scale should be used in a clockwise sense.

Using this protractor, pupils can measure angles to the nearest 10°, or even 5°.

6.74 Learning to use a standard protractor

The difficulties in using a standard, manufactured protractor in the
early stages are that:

The zero line is not the edge of the instrument.

There are two scales, clockwise and anticlockwise.

Divisions marked every degree are visually confusing.

Pupils must be taught to estimate the size of an angle (acute or obtuse)
before measuring it to avoid reading from the wrong scale. They must
then identify which arm of the angle is to serve as zero, to which scale the
0 belongs, and read *round* along this scale. The commonest errors in
using and reading the scales of a protractor are reading from the wrong
scale, and reading a scale in the wrong sense. In this way, a pupil might
give the angle in Fig. 6.24 as 62°, 122° or even 138° (making *both* the
above errors).

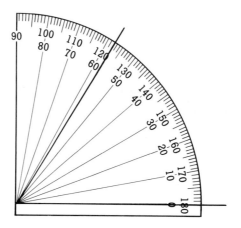

Fig. 6.24

6.8 ANGLE SUM RESULTS

6.81 Angle sum of a triangle

For the following activity, half-used sheets of paper are sufficient.

CLASS ACTIVITY

1 Fold a sheet of paper in half, end-to-end, with the plain side inside the fold.
Open it, and draw a large triangle on one half of the plain side. Try to make
this triangle *scalene*, avoiding special cases such as isosceles or right-angled
ones.

2 Refold the sheet, hold it up to the light, and mark the positions of the three vertices of the triangle on the other half sheet, so as to make an exact copy of the triangle. Cut out the two congruent triangles.

3 On each triangle, letter the angles A, B, C in the same way. From one triangle, tear off the three angles.

4 Arrange the torn-off angles to form a straight line; paste this arrangement beside the other triangle in an exercise book (see Fig. 6.25).

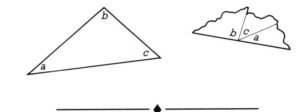

Fig. 6.25

6.82 **Angle sum of a quadrilateral**

Draw a quadrilateral of any shape ; then draw a diagonal, dividing it into two triangles. This leads to the result that the sum of the four interior angles is 360°, or one full turn.

The following activity shows the result in an interesting direct way. Draw an irregular quadrilateral (no equal sides and no right angles). Copy it on another sheet of paper, by pricking through the vertices with a pin. Do this many times, until you have at least 12 congruent quadrilaterals. On each one, mark the four different angles a, b, c, d. Now arrange them so that they all fit together (see Fig. 6.26). Notice that at each vertex the four different angles meet :

$$a + b + c + d = 360°$$

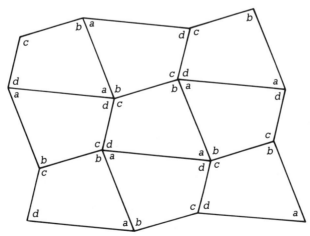

Fig. 6.26

6.9 COORDINATES

If pupils in a classroom are arranged in formal rows at their desks the teacher can show them how to refer to their place with coordinates. Explain with a diagram on the blackboard, but make sure that it is drawn from the pupils' point of view, not the teacher's! Fig. 6.27a shows such a seating plan, with reference letters for each column and numbers for each row. It is often better to introduce the class to the convention 'across, then up' using a letter and a number rather than two numbers. (In some maps, e.g. street maps for large towns, this (letter, number) system is often used.)

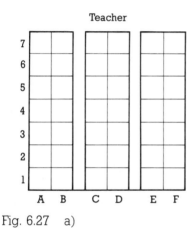

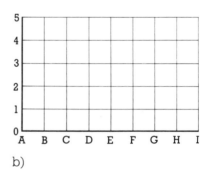

Fig. 6.27   a)   b)

Notice that in this plan, positions are squares. The next step is to introduce the lettering and numbering of *points*: we are labelling the *grid lines*, not the spaces between them (see Fig. 6.27b). Eventually, we introduce the standard coordinate system using pairs of numbers. This is when children must be quite clear that the first number refers to the 'across' scale, the second to the 'up' scale.

(At this stage we are not, of course, concerned with negative numbers; the scales both start with 0 in the bottom left-hand corner.)

Pupils can be given many enjoyable examples, using ordinary squared exercise book paper, teaching them how to plot points and to give their coordinates correctly. Throughout, remember to include points on the axes, with one coordinate 0, and, in particular, the origin (0, 0). As they gain experience, the teacher can introduce the algebraic names *x-coordinate*, *y-coordinate*, and refer to the *x-* and *y-axes*.

6.91 Introductory activities

Dot-to-dot drawings

In a dot-to-dot drawing pupils are given a list of coordinates ; each point must be joined to the next in the list with a ruler. After they have drawn two or three such pictures, they can make some up for themselves, and give them to each other.

Buried treasure

The teacher has a large map of an island (drawn on the blackboard, or on a large sheet of card), with a coordinate grid over it, as shown in Fig. 6.28. Somewhere on the island is buried treasure, filling one square.

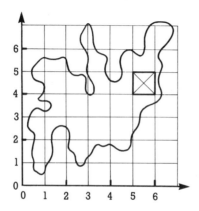

Fig. 6.28

Pupils take turns to name a point which might be one of the corners of this square ; if correct, the teacher marks it on the map. Once one corner has been found, the others should follow quickly and then the treasure can be 'dug up'.

6.10 EXERCISES

1 Describe each of the following shapes. Make a list of the specialised words that you use in each case.

i)	Parallelogram	iii)	Cuboid
ii)	Rhombus	iv)	Pyramid

2 Fold a piece of paper three times : then cut it to make a pattern which has 4 axes of symmetry, and quarter-turn symmetry.

3 Make a paper square. By folding this several times, and then making just *one* straight cut, make a regular octagon.

4 Make a list of at least ten examples in your everyday life where you turn something. In each case, estimate roughly the size of the rotation involved, e.g. *turning a door handle – about half a right angle.*

5 In the regular pentagram (see Fig. 6.13), how many different *shapes* of triangle are there? Of each shape, how many different *sizes* are there? How many triangles are there of each shape and size?

6 Sketch nets for each of the prisms (not the cylinder) shown in Fig. 6.17.

7 The net of a cube consists of six squares. Fig. 6.29 shows two completely different ones; can you draw others? (It is helpful to sketch them on squared paper.)

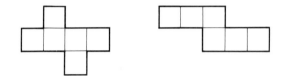

Fig. 6.29

8 Describe how, using models of polyhedra, you might teach a lesson on *horizontal* and *vertical*. Remember that the term may apply to edges as well as to faces, and that a polyhedron can rest on many different faces.

9 Referring to Fig. 6.30, complete the shapes and give the coordinates of the missing vertices:

i)   Parallelogram ABCD   iii) Isosceles trapezium JKLM
ii) Square EFGH   iv)   Rectangle PQRS

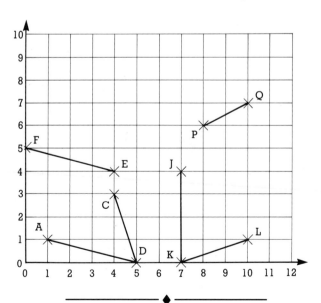

Fig. 6.30

6.101 Hints and answers

2 The folds must make 45° angles at their intersection.

3 Fold as in (2). Then cut across the 45° angle to make 8 isosceles triangles.

4 Control knobs on electrical appliances, radios, etc., taps, wheels, hinges on doors, windows, etc.

5 Two shapes; acute-angled – 3 sizes (5 of the smallest, 10 medium-sized, 5 large); obtuse-angled – 2 sizes (5 small, 10 large).

7 There are 11 different nets.

9 i)   B(0, 4)
 ii) G(1, 9), H(5, 8)
 iii) M(10, 3)
 iv) Several possible answers, e.g.   (10, 2) and (12, 3), (7, 8) and (9, 9)

CHAPTER SEVEN

Perimeter, Area and Volume

7.1 INTRODUCTION

The measurement of shapes, in both two and three dimensions, is known as *mensuration*. For plane figures, this usually includes *perimeter* and *area*. For solids, mensuration includes finding their *surface area* and *volume*. In this chapter we show how these concepts can be developed in the classroom, as general ideas and through the study of specific geometrical shapes.

7.2 PERIMETER

Note It is important not to teach about perimeter and area in the same lesson.

Perimeter is the name given to the distance all the way round the boundary of a figure and is, therefore, one aspect of length. Perimeters of simple figures can be introduced in the early stages of the development of length (see Chapter 5, pp. 100–9).

Unfortunately, teachers often restrict children's experience of perimeter to rectangular figures. They should point out that *circumference* is a special term for the perimeter of a circle.

Here are some other examples where pupils could measure perimeter:

The school compound
Flower beds inside the compound
A classroom block, or other building
The classroom floor
The blackboard
A clock face.

Although some of these are likely to be rectangular, others may be circular, or irregular.

7.21 Perimeter of a rectangle

Because of its symmetry, the rectangle has two pairs of equal sides. To find its perimeter, therefore, pupils need make only two measurements, the *length* and *width* (*breadth*). Each must be doubled and these doubled measurements are then added. (Alternatively, add the two side lengths together and *then* double the sum.)

CLASS ACTIVITY

Rectangles with equal perimeters

1 Using squared paper, each pupil (or each pair of pupils) draws a rectangle with a given perimeter. Suitable perimeters can range from 12 to 24, and should be an even number of units. (The unit is the side of the square.) Children can be given different perimeters for this exercise. The teacher must check that their rectangles have the correct perimeter.

2 Ask the pupils to draw as many different rectangles as they can with the same perimeter. Using only a whole number of units, there is a limited number of such rectangles. One of them may be a square, which is a special kind of rectangle. (Some pupils may include congruent rectangles twice – see the example shown in Fig. 7.1.)

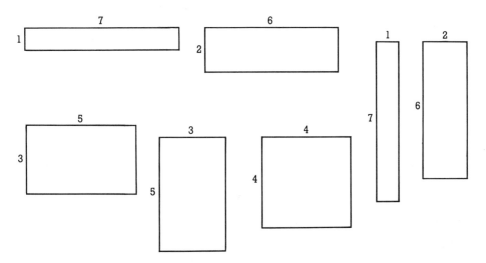

Fig. 7.1

3 Children's work can be displayed on the classroom wall in table form.

Length l	Breadth b	$l + b$	Perimeter
7	1	8	16
6	2	8	16
5	3	8	16
4	4	8	16

By definition, the length must be more than the breadth (or, in the case of a square, equal to it).

Extension

Ask the pupils if measurements could be in half-units or even smaller fractions. In this way they can begin to understand there is no end to the number of different rectangles having the same perimeter.

———————◆———————

CLASS ACTIVITY

Ominoes

An *omino* or *polyomino* is a shape made from equal squares which are *properly connected*, i.e. joined side-to-side and not corner-to-corner. Fig. 7.2a is properly connected, Fig. 7.2b is not. Fig. 7.2a is an example of a *pentomino*, an omino made from *five* squares.

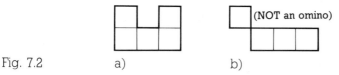

Fig. 7.2   a)   b)

Show pupils an omino which has a perimeter of, say, 12 units. Ask them to draw as many different ones as they can which have the same perimeter.

———————◆———————

7.22   Triangles with a given perimeter

The lengths of any two sides of a triangle must, added together, be greater than the third. When pupils are taught to construct triangles using ruler and compasses, given the three side lengths, they should discover this. If side lengths are restricted to an exact number of centimetres, then there is a limit to the number of different triangles which can be drawn for a given perimeter.

CLASS ACTIVITY

1 Ask pupils to draw, using ruler and compasses, an equilateral triangle with a perimeter of, say, 15 cm.

2 Then ask them to draw another triangle with the same perimeter, and with each of its side lengths an exact number of centimetres.

3 Ask, 'How many different triangles could you draw?' This should lead pupils to some discussion of all the possible side lengths. (The table below shows how, for a perimeter of 15 cm, there are only seven possible triangles. No side can be more than 7 cm long, because otherwise the two remaining sides would together be shorter.)

Side 1	Side 2	Side 3
7	7	1
7	6	2
7	5	3
7	4	4
6	6	3
6	5	4
5	5	5

Note This exercise provides valuable practice in construction work as well as some good number investigation.

———————————◆———————————

7.23 Perimeter (circumference) of a circle

Long before pupils are taught about the circumference of a circle they should have measured the distance round circular objects, at an early stage of length work. They should also have measured roughly circular things, such as their waists, using some kind of tape measure or piece of string.

Measuring diameters

The obvious way to compare the sizes of different circles, or cylindrical objects with circular ends, is by measuring their *diameters*. Depending on the object, we can do this in various ways.

1 Draw round an object on squared paper. If standard graph paper is available, with 1 mm, 2 mm or 5 mm rulings, then the measure of the diameter can be found directly in millimetres or centimetres.

2 Place a ruler directly across the circle. A perspex ruler is best to use, as the whole circle can be seen through the ruler and the widest distance judged more exactly.

3 For a cylindrical object, place parallel faces of flat objects against opposite sides and measure the distance between them : this is the principle on which *calipers* work. Stand the cylinder on squared paper but, for a very long or a fixed cylinder (e.g. a flagpole) it is best to arrange some rectangular objects round it. Fig. 7.3 shows a long tube with three rigid boxes placed against it. You can see that the diameter is measured by finding the distance between the two parallel boxes.

Fig. 7.3

Measuring circumference

To measure the circumference of a cylindrical object there are, again, several different methods.

1 Mark a point on the rim of the cylinder ; then roll it carefully along a straight line, taking care that the cylinder does not slip while rolling. When the mark comes into contact with the line again, the cylinder has completed one full turn. Measure the distance it has travelled. If possible, measure the distance for two or more full turns and take an average.

2 Wind a piece of thread several times (five or ten, if possible) round the cylinder. Then measure the length of thread used (and divide by five or ten).

3 Wrap a piece of lined or squared paper round the cylinder. Mark the length of the wrap on the paper, then unwrap it and use the printed lines to measure the length.

4 To measure a circular hole, roll a sheet of paper into a tube, place the tube in the hole and let it expand to fill the hole. Mark where the edge of the sheet overlaps. Open the sheet and measure the distance from the edge to the mark.

Comparing circumference and diameter

Pupils should discover the relationship that

the circumference of a circle is a little more than three times the diameter.

The teacher can lead them to this recovery in various ways depending on how the circumference has been measured. For example, using method (1) above, three diameters can be placed end-to-end to show that the distance rolled is a bit more than this. If thread is wrapped round the cylinder (method (2)), then the length of thread can be marked on a table top. Use the cylinder itself to measure this distance, using the diameter as a unit of length. If the thread was wrapped round five times, then the total thread length should be about 16 diameters. Using method (3), with a strip of paper wrapped round the cylinder the actual diameter can again be used as a unit. Alternatively, measure the diameter as described on p. 150. For larger circles, such as washing bowls, buckets, wheels, measure the circumference and diameter using standard units and the methods described above.

Fig. 7.4 shows that the circumference is more than $3 \times d$ (or rather, $6 \times r$). The regular hexagon has sides equal in length to the radius r of the circle, so its perimeter is $6r$, or $3d$.

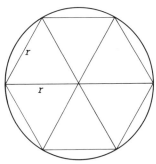

Fig. 7.4

The sides of the hexagon join points of the circle with straight lines, so the perimeter of the circle is obviously slightly more than that of the hexagon.

CLASS ACTIVITY

The class should be divided into groups, each consisting of three or four pupils.

1 Each group should be given a different circular object to measure. Different groups can be given different methods to use, as suggested above.

2 The measurements of the groups are recorded by the teacher on the blackboard, and copied by each pupil into his or her exercise book. This is an example for neat tabulation.

Object	Diameter d cm	Circumference c cm	$3d$	$c \div d$

Note The aim is first to compare c with $3d$ – this only involves multiplication by 3. Later, when the class are confident with decimal work and long division, they can work out $c \div d$ in each case. The working should be carried to, at most, two decimal places. This stage can be omitted if the pupils are not ready for it.

———————————◆———————————

Proportionality

Another way of expressing the relationship between c and d is to say that

the circumference is proportional to the diameter

This means, in simple terms, that doubling the diameter also doubles the circumference: if one circle has diameter 5 cm and another 8 cm, then their circumferences will also be in the ratio 5 : 8. This is best shown by making a graph. Using actual objects such as lids, reels, etc., mark their diameters on the horizontal axis (you can draw round the objects showing at least half of their circumference as in Fig. 7.5). Then wrap thread round each one using a small knot in the thread as starting point, and to hold on to while wrapping. Cut the thread off to measure exactly one turn. Then fasten this thread length to the paper with glue in a vertical direction at the end of the appropriate diameter.

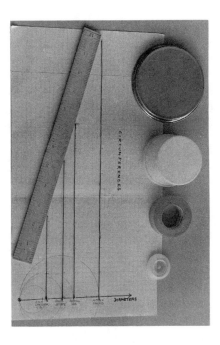

Fig. 7.5

Notice that the ends of the threads lie roughly in a straight line – this is how the graph shows that *c* is *directly proportional* to *d*. The straight line, when extended to the bottom of the graph, should pass through the origin, O.

Note   This is a practical experiment, so pupils' results may not show a perfect straight line. This illustrates again that all measurement is approximate.

The number π

The ancient Greek mathematicians discovered that the ratio $\dfrac{\text{circumference}}{\text{diameter}}$ was the same for any circle. They gave this number the name π (pi, the Greek letter p). The value of π cannot be written using decimals or fractions because *it is not a rational number*. This may seem strange, since it is the value of a ratio. The value of π is *approximately* $3\frac{1}{7}$ or 3.14 : the first of these is actually too large, and the second too small, but for most school work they are good enough approximations. (The first twenty decimal places for π are

$$3.141\ 592\ 653\ 589\ 793\ 238\ 46\ldots$$

and we could go on writing decimal digits for ever without any pattern appearing. This is true of all irrational numbers.)

It is remarkable that, over 2200 years ago, Archimedes stated that π was less than $3\frac{10}{70}$ and more than $3\frac{10}{71}$: that is,

$$3\frac{10}{71} < \pi < 3\frac{10}{70}$$

Remembering that the Greeks did not use our place-value system or have our simple way of writing fractions, this was a truly remarkable result, showing that Archimedes must be reckoned amongst the greatest mathematicians of all time.

7.3 AREA

Area is a measure of surface – the amount of land within a boundary, the surface of water in a lake, the amount of carpet needed to cover a floor, or of material to make a certain dress pattern. The space whose area we are measuring is often flat; if it is not flat, e.g. the curved surface of a cylinder or a cone, or curtain material which has been gathered, then we need to flatten it in order to measure its area.

For this reason, children should be introduced to area in a variety of situations – not just the area of a rectangle drawn on a blackboard ! The stages of development then follow the same sequence as with length, mass and capacity (see Chapter 5).

7.31 Language and vocabulary

Show pupils two objects which are quite different in shape, e.g. two leaves from different plants. Ask them, 'Which leaf is the larger one ?' They will probably first compare their lengths, or widths. The teacher can then, if necessary, guide the pupils to compare the 'amount of green', i.e. the areas. They should then be able to say, 'The area of this one is more than the area of that one', 'This one has the greater area', and so on.

7.32 Conservation of area

Children must understand that, if a shape is divided into small pieces and these are then rearranged to make a different shape, the final shape has the same area as the first. Here are some examples.

a) Tear a sheet of paper into several smaller rectangles, and use these to make various new shapes.

b) Tangrams are an ancient Chinese recreation, using seven pieces cut from a large square (see Fig. 7.6a). These pieces can be rearranged in many different ways (see Fig. 7.6b)

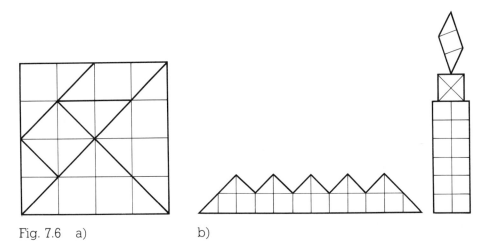

Fig. 7.6   a)   b)

CLASS ACTIVITY

Pentominoes

A pentomino is an omino with five squares (see p. 148).

Children should work in small groups of three or four. Each group should have at least ten equal squares cut from thin card. (If wooden or plastic squares are available, these can be used.) Each pupil should also have some squared paper.

Fig. 7.7

Show the class how there are only two different *trominoes* using three squares (see Fig. 7.7). Then ask how many 4-square ominoes (tetrominoes) they can make: it should not take long for the class to discover all five shown in Fig. 7.8. Pupils should then draw all of them on squared paper.

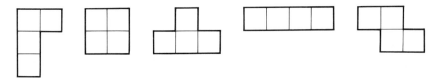

Fig. 7.8

Now show the class two different pentominoes such as those in Fig. 7.9 (overleaf). Ask the pupils to draw these on a new sheet of squared paper. Then ask each group to find as many different pentominoes as they can. Encourage them to turn shapes round, noting that they remain the same shape even

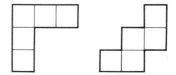

Fig. 7.9

though seen from a different position. If the class begins to tire, tell them that there are only twelve different pentominoes, and challenge each group to find them all. Note that the 12 different pentominoes have a total area of 60 unit squares. They can be fitted together in many different ways to make a rectangle, measuring 6×10, 5×12, 4×15 or 3×20. Fig. 7.10 shows one of these arrangements.

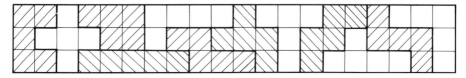

Fig. 7.10

---◆---

7.33 Comparison

Two shapes which are flat and can be cut out, or traced, can have their areas compared by laying, or drawing, one of them on top of the other. The shapes of different provinces or countries on a map can be compared this way as can two leaves. This can be extended to three or more shapes, ordering them according to their area.

7.34 Using non-standard units

Pupils soon come to realise that squares are the most convenient unit of area. However, rectangles also work well (or, indeed, any geometrical shapes that will *tessellate* – that is, fit together without leaving spaces in between). Use match boxes to cover different areas: on an appropriate map it can be shown that Ghana is more than twice the area of Liberia.

Although they do not tessellate, circles can be used to obtain reasonable comparison. By using coins or bottle tops, pupils will realise that circles are less satisfactory than rectangles or squares because they leave spaces between them.

When they appreciate the convenience of squares, pupils should compare some of the shapes which they have looked at earlier by drawing round, or tracing, them on squared paper: standard 6 mm ruling in exercise books is quite good for this.

This exercise should not involve too much counting. Discuss what to do about 'bits' – squares which are only partly inside the boundary. Group these together to make up wholes (see Fig. 7.11) ; later, agree to count as 'half' any square which is between $\frac{1}{4}$ and $\frac{3}{4}$ inside the boundary.

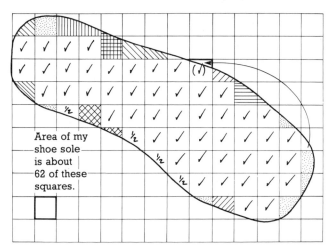

Fig. 7.11

Then suggest :

If a square is *less than half* inside, *do not count* it ;
If a square is *half or more than half* inside, *count* it.

Children will accept this as reasonable, once they understand that even quite large bits which fail to qualify are matched by other just over half squares, which do get counted. In Fig. 7.12a, the squares labelled a and b would not be counted, but c and d would be counted. We can see that Sudan is about four times the area of Kenya, and nearly three times the area of Tanzania. Tanzania is about $1\frac{1}{2}$ times the area of Kenya, or 'half as big again'.

Area of a rectangle
Pupils may discover that the counting process could be shortened by grouping squares in equal rows or columns. For example, in Fig. 7.12b (overleaf), the area within the heavy line is seen as three rows of five squares, i.e. 3×5 squares. In this tracing of Sudan, the scale and the square size are the same as in Fig. 7.12a. However, because the grid is in a slightly different position over the map, the square count is likely to give a slightly different result. This emphasises the approximate nature of the method. If the unit square is small enough in relation to the area of

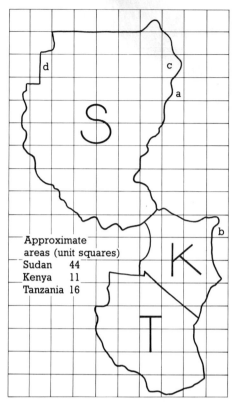

Fig. 7.12   a)   b)

the shapes being measured, the results of different counts should be approximately the same.

So far, there has been no mention of any unit of length in area work – the side of the unit squares has not been considered. The ground has, therefore, now been prepared for the introduction of the standard unit, the *square centimetre*.

7.35   Standard units of area

The basic unit of length is the *metre*, so the basic unit of area is the metre square (with a side length of one metre) : its area is *one square metre* (1 m^2). It is essential that pupils should see and experience this unit. A metre square can be made easily using sheets of newspaper, especially if the sheets measure 60 cm by 40 cm.

Square centimetres

For desk-top purposes the square metre is much too large. One metre is 100 centimetres, so a metre square contains 100×100 centimetre squares: $1 \text{ m}^2 = 10\,000 \text{ cm}^2$. This is a very large number, so it is essential in area work to use only one unit at a time.

In the classroom, it is desirable to have some paper ruled in square centimetres, but this may not be readily available. Standard school graph paper, ruled at 2 mm intervals, usually has heavier lines printed every centimetre; this can therefore be used, and the fainter lines ignored.

Hectares

A hectometre is 100 metres, so the *hectare* (square hectometre) is the area of a square with side length 100 m. This is the standard unit of land measure, e.g. a farm or a building plot. The square hectometre contains 100×100 metre squares, so

$$1 \text{ ha} = 10\,000 \text{ m}^2$$

Note. On a map with a scale of 1 : 10 000, 1 cm² represents 1 ha. This scale of map is sometimes available, showing urban areas in great detail.

To calculate an area in hectares, it is often easiest to think of lengths in 100 m (i.e. hectometre) units. For example, a rectangular plot measuring 320 m by 85 m is 3.2 hm by 0.85 hm; its area is therefore (3.2×0.85) ha.

7.36   Standard plane figures (polygons)

A rectangle measuring a units of length by b units can be filled with a rows of unit squares, each row containing b squares. Its area is therefore $a \times b$ unit squares. This leads to the standard result for the *area of a rectangle*:

$$area = length \times breadth$$

Using this the area of many *rectilinear* figures can be calculated; such figures can be divided into rectangles as in Fig. 7.13.

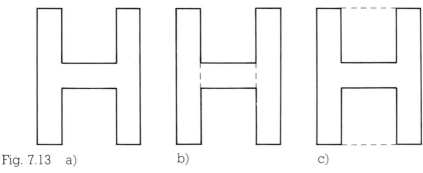

Fig. 7.13   a)   b)   c)

Note here that there are two ways of obtaining the area of the 'H'. The more obvious one, which all pupils would naturally use to start with, is to divide it into three rectangles (see Fig. 7.13b) and then add their areas together. Often, however, a subtraction method can be used, and with experience pupils can be introduced to this: in some cases it makes for quicker working. In Fig. 7.13c, the 'H' can be seen to be a large rectangle with two equal smaller ones cut away.

Vocabulary

Certain common words which are used in connection with plane figures are not always descriptive. These standard terms need to be explained carefully. For example, the 'height' of a triangle drawn on a flat sheet of paper cannot mean the same thing as the height of a tree. Similarly, the word 'base' suggests a surface, in contact with the ground, and a three-dimensional object rather than a plane figure; we do, in fact, use 'base' when talking of the volume of a prism – 'base area multiplied by height'.

The same confusion can also exist with solids. A cylinder with its axis horizontal, such as a length of piping or a cylindrical tin lying on a table (rather than standing) has circular *ends* and a *length* (of the axis). Where are its *base* and *height*?

There is no substitute for practical experience with objects. Children should handle them and talk about them. In this way they gain a deeper understanding of the concepts which are involved.

Area of a triangle

Any rectangle can be divided into two congruent, right-angled triangles by drawing a diagonal. The area of each triangle is therefore half of the rectangle. Pupils should cut out two congruent rectangles and then cut one of them along a diagonal. The three pieces can then be pasted into an exercise book.

Mark any point on one of the longer sides of a rectangle, and join it to the two other corners (see Fig. 7.14a). In this way three triangles are formed, two of them right-angled. Again, pupils should cut out two congruent rectangles, mark points and join lines on each in exactly the same position, and then cut one of the rectangles into three pieces. They can discover for themselves that the two right-angled triangles exactly cover the third triangle. The area of this triangle is, therefore, half that of the rectangle.

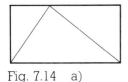 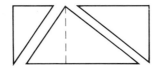 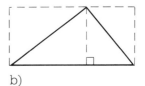

Fig. 7.14   a)   b)

If we make the longest side of a triangle its base, then we can always draw
a rectangle with this base as its length; the height of the triangle is the
breadth of the rectangle (see Fig. 7.14b). Note that the *height*, or
altitude, of the triangle is *perpendicular to the base*. The more
specialised word 'altitude' may be better in this context, even though it
simply means height. Every triangle, therefore, has an area half that of a
rectangle. If children experience the matching of the equal areas as
suggested, they will understand the result for the *area of a triangle*:

$$area = \tfrac{1}{2}\,(base \times altitude)$$

Area of a parallelogram

This is the simplest way to make a parallelogram.

1   Draw a rectangle and cut it out (or use a rectangular piece of paper).

2   Draw an oblique line from one corner to make a right-angled triangle
    (see Fig. 7.15a).

3   Cut off this triangle, and move it to the other end of the rectangle (see
    Fig. 7.15b).

 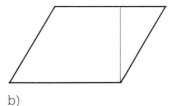

Fig. 7.15   a)   b)

The area of the parallelogram must be equal to that of the rectangle. For
the parallelogram shown in Fig. 7.15b, it would be reasonable to talk of
its length and breadth. But this would not always be so, e.g. in Fig. 7.16a.
The terminology is made clear if we stress that the height or *altitude* of
the figure is the *distance between* one pair of parallel sides. Distance in
geometry always implies shortest distance, i.e. by a perpendicular. The
area of a parallelogram can be remembered as:

(length of one side) × *(distance between sides with that length)*

It is important for pupils to experience many parallelograms, with different proportions and angles, and in different positions. They should be able to identify both altitudes for any parallelogram (see Fig. 7.16b).

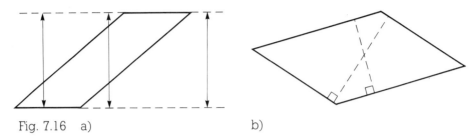

Fig. 7.16   a)   b)

Area of a trapezium

There are several good ways of showing the area of a trapezium. A class might discover more than one of these different groups working in different ways.

CLASS ACTIVITY

1 Give each pupil a sheet of lined paper. Ask each one to draw a trapezium, using the printed lines to make the two parallel sides; tell them to make sure that these parallel sides are separated by an *even* number of spaces (4, 6 or 8 are convenient numbers, giving trapeziums of about the right size for this work).

2 Now ask each pupil to make an exact copy of the trapezium, by cutting the first one out and carefully drawing round it (or pricking at the vertices). Cut the second trapezium out as well. On each, label the lengths of the parallel sides *a* and *b*, and the distance between them *h*.

3 The pupils can now be arranged in groups. Each group follows just *one* of the following methods.

Method A

Use your two trapeziums to make a parallelogram.

    What is the length or base of the parallelogram?
    What is the width or 'height' (altitude)?
    What is the area of the parallelogram?
    What is the area of each trapezium (see Fig. 7.17)?

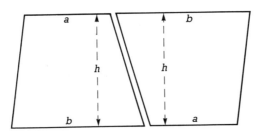

Fig. 7.17

Method B

Cut one trapezium along the half-way line, i.e. the line parallel to the parallel sides, half-way up the trapezium (see Fig. 7.18). Arrange the two pieces to make a parallelogram.

What is the length or base of the parallelogram?
What is the width or height (altitude)?
What is the area of the parallelogram, and therefore of the trapezium?

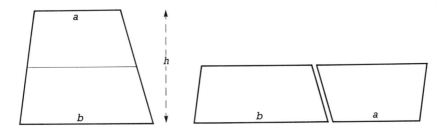

Fig. 7.18

In each case, pupils can paste the pieces into their exercise books – the whole trapezium, and the other pieces in their new arrangement.

Both the methods in this section depend on the *conservation of area* i.e. when pieces of a shape are rearranged, the total area is unchanged.

7.37   Area of a circle

Fig. 7.19a (overleaf) shows that the area of a circle of radius r is less than $4r^2$.

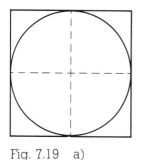 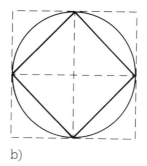 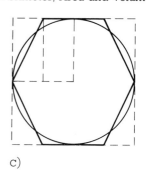

Fig. 7.19   a)   b)   c)

In Fig. 7.19b the inner square has area half that of the outer square. The circle therefore has area more than $2r^2$.

In Fig. 7.19c, the hexagon is formed by cutting away one quarter of each of the squares in Fig. 7.19a – the right-angled triangles at the corners of the large square. This leaves three-quarters of the large square, whose area is $4r^2$: the area of the hexagon is therefore $3r^2$. The area of the circle is clearly roughly equal to this.

Pupils who have already discovered that the circumference of a circle is π times, or 'a little more than 3' times, the diameter might reasonably wonder if, here, the area is also πr^2. The following activity will allow pupils to investigate the relationship in more detail.

CLASS ACTIVITY

Arrange pupils in small groups of two or three. Give each group two circular objects of different sizes, e.g. a coin and a tin lid. Let there be five or six different objects in the class altogether, so that several different groups have identical objects.

Pupils should draw round each of their objects on squared paper, and then find the diameter of each circle, using the square side as unit.

Then they need to find the area of each circle as accurately as they can by counting squares (see p. 156). The results can be presented in a table.

Object	Diameter	Radius r	r^2	$3r^2$	Area A	$A \div r^2$

As with the work on circumference and diameter (see p. 151), the first stage should be to compare $3r^2$ and A, noting that A is in most cases a little more than $3r^2$. Pupils who are confident with decimal work and long division, can work out $A \div r^2$ in each case.

───────────◆───────────

A way of showing that $A = \pi r^2$

The following well-known demonstration of the result can be done by a class, if they have some paper and scissors.

Draw a circle with diameter not more than 12 cm. (For demonstration purposes, the teacher can do this with card, using a much larger circle.) By folding, or by measurement with a protractor, divide the circle into 16 sectors. Colour the arcs of the sectors using two different colours, one for each semicircular arc of the circle (see Fig. 7.20a).

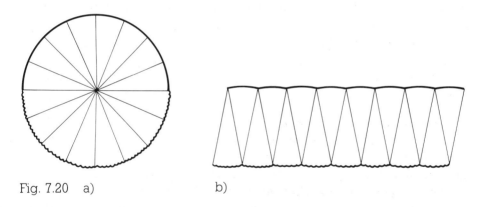

Fig. 7.20   a)   b)

Cut out all the sectors and paste them onto a page of the pupil's exercise book, arranging them head-to-tail as in Fig. 7.20b.

The shape which they make is rather like a parallelogram. Imagine many more sectors – for example, 120, each with an angle of 3° – and we can see that the shape will be almost a rectangle, although its long sides are a bit wavy.

For a circle of radius r, the length of each semicircular arc is πr: this is the length of the parallelogram. The width or height of the parallelogram is the radius r. The area of the parallelogram is therefore $r \times \pi r$, or πr^2. But since the parallelogram is formed from the cut-up pieces of the circle, this is also the area of the circle.

7.38   Surface area of solids

So far, we have only considered areas of shapes which are flat, or nearly flat. We can also find the areas of surfaces of solid objects. We often do this by considering the flattened form of the surface, called a *net*.

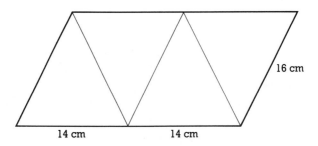

Fig. 7.21

Fig. 7.21 shows the net for a tetrahedron, the shape often used for milk cartons. This net has the shape of a parallelogram ; we can find the area of the net, and this is the surface area of the tetrahedron.

The surface area of any polyhedron – that is, a solid with plane faces and straight edges – can be found by adding together the areas of all the separate faces, whether they are triangles, rectangles or any other shapes.

The curved surface of a cylinder

Labels stuck onto cylindrical tins are rectangular in shape. Pupils should see examples of this for different sizes of tin. They can then be given a tin, and asked how large a label it needs. By experimenting with the tin and a piece of paper, they will discover that the length of the label must be at least equal to the circumference of the tin, and the width of the label slightly less than the height of the tin. A good example of a cylindrical surface is a hollow tube, e.g. from a toilet roll. This can be cut straight from one end to the other ; when flattened, the card is rectangular. Notice, however, that the tube is usually made with a spiral join going round it : if you cut along this spiral, the tube flattens to give a parallelogram. After practical experience of this kind, pupils will understand that the *area of the curved surface of a cylinder* is

circumference of base (or end) × height (or length)

Eventually, they should remember the formula :

Area of curved surface of a cylinder $= (\pi d) \times h$

Other curved surfaces

The cone is a common shape which children should know. It occurs in funnels, spires of buildings, traditional hats and the familiar ice-cream cone. Pupils should be able to make a conical surface from the sector of a circle as shown in Fig. 7.22.

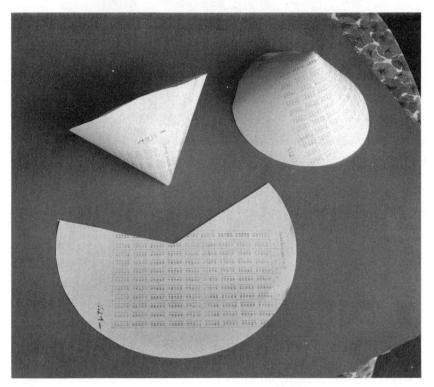

Fig. 7.22

They can experiment with different sectors of the same circle, major and minor. They should notice how the base diameter and the height of the cone change according to the angle of the sector. Obviously if a cone is made from three-quarters of a circle (a sector with angle 270°) its surface area must be three-quarters, or $\frac{270}{360}$, of the area of the circle. This topic is not normally taken any further, however, until secondary school.

A spherical surface cannot be flattened perfectly. However, the area can be found approximately by cutting or tearing it into strips. For example, the surface area of an orange could be found by peeling it, arranging the pieces of peel on a sheet of squared paper, and drawing round the outline (see Fig. 7.23, overleaf).

Fig. 7.23

It is interesting for pupils to try to cover the surface of, say, a football with sheets of thin paper, such as newspaper. They will discover that it cannot be done perfectly but, with patience and a lot of cutting and glue, they can cover the area approximately. They can check their finding with the result:

Area of a sphere $= 4\pi r^2$ (where r is the radius of the sphere)

7.4 VOLUME

A solid object has *volume*, whereas a hollow container has *capacity*. Imagine such a container being filled with liquid wax, or molten metal, which then solidifies: the capacity has been changed into volume. The two concepts are very closely related; the units in which they are measured – millilitres (ml) and cubic centimetres (cm^3) – are equivalent, 1 ml being the capacity of a hollow centimetre cube.

7.41 Conservation of volume

Unfortunately, a supply of unit cubes may not be readily available. If possible, have some made by a carpenter from wood: 2 cm cubes are better to start with than 1 cm ones, but the size does not matter provided that they are all the same. Alternatively, matchboxes or other small cuboids can be used, if enough of them can be found. Give each child in a group the same number of blocks, 12 or 15, perhaps. Ask each child to make a building with them. Which building is the largest? When they understand that something is the same, they are ready to use the word *volume*.

A child, given a lump of soft clay or plasticine, can mould it into different shapes, but each time the volume of clay remains the same. When he or she has grasped this fact, the child has understood that volume is *conserved*.

7.5 **EXERCISES**

1 How many different rectangles can you draw for a given perimeter, using only whole numbers of units for the side lengths? For example, there are 4 different rectangles (1×8, 2×7, 3×6, 4×5) with a perimeter of 18 units. Make a table showing the number, n, of different rectangles with a perimeter of p units, for all even numbers from $p = 16$ to $p = 36$. Can you discover a rule for calculating n from p?

2 Measure the circumference of a cylindrical object by wrapping a length of thin thread round it *ten times*. How accurate do you think your result is? What are the possible reasons for inaccuracy?

3 Fig. 7.24 shows a square and a rectangle which have equal perimeters. Explain why the square has greater area than the rectangle.

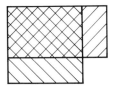

Fig. 7.24

4 How many different cuboids could you build with 24 unit cubes? For each one, calculate the total surface area in unit squares.

5 From a piece of thin card, draw and cut out a large circular sector which is at least a semicircle (see Fig. 7.22). Use it to make a conical surface, fastening it with glue or sticky tape.
Now make a cylindrical tube from another piece of thin card. Make it to have the same base diameter and vertical height as the cone; first measure the height of the cone, to give the correct width for the rectangle you need to cut out, and then find the correct length (the circumference of the base) by trial and error.
Fill the cone with sand and pour the sand into the tube, which should be standing on a flat, even surface. How many times do you need to do this in order to fill the cylindrical tube?

◆

7.51 **Hints and answers**

1 When p is divided by 4, n is the quotient (ignoring the remainder), e.g. for $p = 20$, $n = 5$ and for $p = 22$, $n = 5$.

2 It should be possible to measure the length of thread to the nearest 0.5 cm, giving a result for the circumference to an accuracy of 0.5 mm. Inaccuracies arise if the thread is stretched, either in the wrapping or, afterwards, in the measuring. Also, as the thread is wrapped around it will not form exact circles although, if each turn lies in contact with the previous one, this will make little difference. The usual human errors in measuring will, of course, occur.

3 The rectangle on the right-hand side is smaller than the one at the bottom. Draw the small square which is missing on the bottom right-hand corner: this is needed to make the right-hand rectangle equal to the bottom one.

4 Cuboids $4 \times 3 \times 2$, $6 \times 2 \times 2$, $6 \times 4 \times 1$, $8 \times 3 \times 1$, $12 \times 2 \times 1$. These have surface areas of 52, 56, 68, 70, 74 respectively. Note that the one nearest to being a cube $(4 \times 3 \times 2)$ has the smallest surface area.

5 This activity requires time and patience, but it should demonstrate that the cone has about one-third of the volume of the cylinder.

CHAPTER EIGHT

Time, Speed and Rates

8.1 TIME

Our concept of time arises from our awareness of change; without change in the things around us – the position of the sun, the growth of plants, the habits of people and animals – there would be no time. We can measure time by observing and comparing the regularity of such changes.

We can begin to develop children's awareness of time by drawing their attention to activities, ones which occur regularly in their daily lives such as bed-time, school-time, breakfast-time, time to go home, day and night, birthdays and other special days.

Also the teacher should use frequently the vocabulary of time:

now, then, before, after, when, next, sometime, never, morning, afternoon, evening, yesterday, today, tomorrow, weekend, week, month, year, day, hour, minute, second, slow, fast, how long?

Regular events in the pupils' school day can be shown in picture form, e.g. rising in the morning, washing, getting dressed, eating breakfast, going to school, etc. Children can be asked to arrange these pictures in sequence; they can then make statements or answer questions about them, e.g.

After I eat breakfast, I walk to school. Then I play with my friends.
What do you do before you go to school?

FOR THE TEACHER TO MAKE

A water timer

1 Use a nail, or some other sharp object, to make a small hole in the side of a tin can, just above its base. Plug the hole from the outside with a twisted scrap of paper.

2 Stand the can on a smaller object, such as another can, inside a bowl or dish (see Fig. 8.1, overleaf).

Fig. 8.1

3 Fill the can with water and then remove the plug; the water will run out into the bowl in the same time on each occasion. A plastic bottle, through which the water level can be seen, can be used instead of the tin can. Mark two levels on it above the hole; the time taken for the water to fall from one mark to the other can be used as the unit of time.

———————◆———————

Use the timer to find how often an activity can be repeated in the fixed time, e.g.

A pupil jumping on the spot.
Signing your name on a sheet of paper.
Tying a knot in a piece of string.
Threading beads on a string.

Ask pupils to close their eyes: can they guess when all the water has run out?

8.11 Days of the week
Pupils should soon learn the days of the week, and the sequence which they follow. Fig. 6.20a, p. 137 shows a simple learning aid, giving the cycle of days and showing how it continues endlessly. The English names

of the days come from the 'heavenly bodies' – the Sun, the Moon and Saturn – and the ancient Norse gods Tiw, Woden, Thor and Freya. The reasons for having seven days in a week are religious, not astronomical.

8.12   The calendar – months and days

Our modern calendar is known as the Julian calendar, named after the Roman Julius Caesar. The original Roman calendar had ten months: the names September, October, November and December come from the Latin words for 7, 8, 9 and 10. January, the month which looks back at the old year and forward to the new, was named after Janus, the god with two faces who looked in both directions. July and August were named after the Caesars Julius and Augustus, who were born in those months.

FOR THE TEACHER TO MAKE

A wall calendar

You need a large rectangular sheet of card, and two smaller pieces of card, contrasting in colour if possible.

1 Using the rim or lid of a large pan, or other object, cut two discs from the smaller pieces of card, and find their centres.

2 Using a protractor, draw twelve radii at 30° intervals on one disc. On the other disc, mark thirty points round the edge at 12° intervals.

3 Write the month names along the radii of the first disc, the right-hand one in Fig. 8.2. Write the numerals 1–30 by the edge of the second disc. (31 can be written alongside 1, and covered over for months containing 30 or fewer days.)

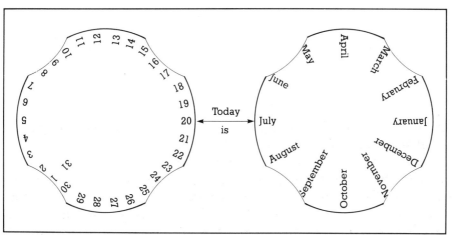

Fig. 8.2

4 Place the two discs side by side on the rectangular sheet, and draw lightly round them. Cut 'tongues' in the sheet to hold the discs in position, but allowing them to be turned freely. Insert the discs under the tongues.

5 Indicate the date as shown in Fig. 8.2.

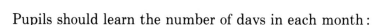

Pupils should learn the number of days in each month:

Thirty days have September,
April, June and November,
All the rest have thirty-one
Except for February alone
Which has but twenty-eight days clear
And twenty-nine in each Leap Year.

The months with 31 days can be remembered by using a 'knuckle calendar' (see Fig. 8.3) : hold the fists as shown and name the knuckles and dips between them, starting from the left. The dips are the months with fewer than 31 days.

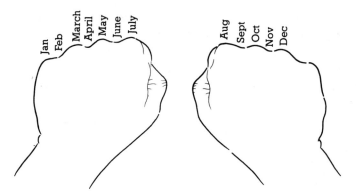

Fig. 8.3

The month is, roughly, the time taken for the Moon to orbit the Earth, i.e. about 30 days. The ancient Chaldeans counted the year as 360 days (12×30). In fact, the time taken for the Earth to orbit the Sun is about $365\frac{1}{4}$ days, and so we have to adjust our calendar occasionally – hence our leap years. Even then our present calendar is not perfect. When the Gregorian calendar was introduced in 1752 by jumping forward eleven days there were riots ; in London and other places, people demanded, 'Give us back our eleven days !'

By counting 365 days in the year, we lose about $\frac{1}{4}$ day and so have to make this up by having an extra day every fourth year. For convenience we do this at the end of February, in any year which is a multiple of 4. So, in 1988, 1992, 1996, . . . February is 29 days long.

Note Because the true astronomical year is not exactly $365\frac{1}{4}$ days, we do not have leap years in the century years – 1700, 1800, 1900. But, to make for even finer adjustment, the year 2000 will be a leap year !

8.13 Hours and minutes – telling the time

Nowadays, digital clocks and watches are as common as the older analogue type, with hands rotating over a circular face, but pupils should still be introduced to the time of day through the traditional clock face. Older, historical ways of recording the time of day, such as sundials, water clocks or the steady burning of a large candle, are interesting and might be investigated once children understand the conventional clock.

Children learn to tell the time in stages. But first, try to show them, with a real clock, how the hands are always moving – even the hour hand is creeping round the face, in the same direction as the minute hand. As the long hand completes one revolution, so the short hand moves on from one numeral to the next.

The following progression can be followed using a demonstration clock made from cardboard.

1 *Hours*: Show how the short (*hour*) hand points exactly at the numerals on the hour and between them at other times.

2 *Hours and half-hours*: Add the long hand to the face.

   a Point the long (*minute*) hand at 12, and teach the *o'clocks*.

   b Point the long hand at 6, and teach the *half-pasts*; make sure that the short hand is half-way between the hour numerals.

3 *Quarter past and quarter to*: Take great care to position the short hand correctly. Ask pupils, 'Has the short hand just gone *past* a number, or is it about to go *to* the next number (see Fig. 8.4)?

Fig. 8.4   Quarter past 7   Quarter to 11

4 To introduce the other times a rubber-stamp clock face (without hands) is ideal. The teacher can use this in exercise books or on worksheets.

   a Draw hands in position, and ask pupils to tell the time.
   b State a time, and ask pupils to draw the hands correctly.

5 Now teach 'official' or *digital* times. This may also be done in stages. First use only 15, 30 and 45; establish that 'quarter past' is 15 (past), 'half past' is 30 (past) and 'quarter to' is 45 (past).

Later, pupils will learn to estimate times between the 5 minute intervals, e.g. 3.17 and 8.54. They also learn about a.m. and p.m. (Latin – *ante* and *post meridiem*, meaning *before* and *after midday*). Teachers should contrast this international way of giving local times with traditional ones, e.g. counting the hours from dawn to dusk, and starting again through the night.

8.14 Seconds

Children learn that 60 minutes make an hour. But for a young child even a minute can seem quite a long time; to estimate the duration of a minute, they need to be able to count a smaller unit. We can do this with a pendulum.

CLASSROOM ACTIVITY

The pendulum

You need some thin string, cut into lengths of about 1.5 m, and a supply of bottle tops which have had holes punched through them (or an alternative bob for the pendulum).

1 Working in groups of three or more, pupils thread bottle tops onto a length of string. Some groups should have more tops on their string than others – the number on a string might vary from four to ten. Tie the tops together at one end of the string, to form the bob of a pendulum.

2 Groups, who have different sized bobs on their string, should hold their pendulums with the same length of string between hand and bob, and set them swinging with small swings.
   Note that the pendulums 'beat' at approximately the same rate however large the bobs are. (The beat of the pendulum is the time taken to swing from one side to the other.)

3 Now compare the beats of the pendulums when the amplitude – the width of each swing – is varied. Again, *the beat is the same for different amplitudes.* Ask the class, 'What happens when you move your hand, and change the length of string?' They will discover that:

   The longer the string is, the slower the beat.

A pendulum of a fixed length beats at the same rate, whatever

(a) the weight of the bob
(b) the amplitude of the swing (see Fig. 8.5).

Only the length of the pendulum affects the time of swing.

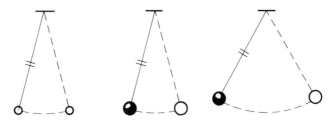

Fig. 8.5

4 The teacher should now find a suitable point to hang one of the pendulums, and make the length, from hanging point to bob, one metre. (The most suitable place to suspend a pendulum may be from a roof timber. This is often easiest outside a classroom, under a verandah. A low branch of a tree could also be used. However, try to find a suitable point inside the classroom, so that the pendulum can be kept there permanently.)

─────────── ◆ ───────────

   It is a most useful (and easily remembered) result that a pendulum of length one metre beats seconds with sufficient accuracy for any classroom work. The teacher can therefore set up a seconds pendulum as described above for reference in the classroom.

   To make children familiar with seconds and short periods of time, up to a minute, there are several simple activities using a seconds pendulum. The teacher should also have a clock or watch which can be used for timing one minute. (Ideally, there should be a clock which all the class can see.) For these activities, pupils should work in pairs: one child keeps the time, counting the beats of the pendulum, while the other does the activity.

a) Breathe steadily and naturally; time one minute (or half a minute), and count how many breaths you take. Then estimate a minute by counting your breaths.

b) Watch the pendulum beating and count quietly, 'Beat-one, beat-two, beat-three, beat-four, . . .' in time. Counting in this way, estimate 10 seconds. Then estimate longer periods, e.g. 20 seconds, half a minute, and a whole minute. (When you get beyond 'beat-twelve' it may be easier to say, 'thir-teen, four-teen, fif-teen, . . ., etc.')

c) Estimate how long it would take to walk right round the classroom block, or some other distance, e.g. from the door to the school office. Then walk, and see how accurate your estimate was.

d) How long does it take you to write your full name? Write your name ten times, and time this accurately; then divide the time by 10.

8.15   Time calculations

The units of time are the only ones in regular, everyday use which are not decimals: that is, the groupings of units are not in tens, hundreds and thousands. For this reason, pupils have to be very careful when calculating with them. Column headings, stating the units, should always be used, e.g.

w d	h m	m s
5 3	10 35	1 22
+ 2 5	− 8 50	× 4

Note that there are few realistic situations which lead to computation of this kind. In particular, it should not be necessary to include examples which use more than two different units.

The most important type of calculation is of the length of a period of time – the *duration* of a journey, a school term, and so on. In these cases, *subtraction* is involved and the best method is often to add on (complementary addition – see Section 3.47, p. 52).

Consider, for example, the subtraction above; this would be needed to answer the question:

How long is it from the start of the second period at 8.50 to the break at 10.35?

Answer in this way:

From 8.50 to 9.00 is 10 minutes. From 9.00 to 10.35 is 1 hour 35 minutes. The total duration is therefore 1 hour 45 minutes.

If pupils are trained to work with time in this way, treating it quite differently from other computation, they are less likely to make decimal errors, e.g. subtracting 8.50 from 10.35 and giving 1 h 85 m as the answer.

8.16 Timetables

In the upper primary school pupils should learn how to read the 24 hour clock, which is used in bus, train and air timetables. A demonstration clock as shown in Fig. 8.6 will be useful. To conform with standard, international notation the hours should be written using four digits:

01.00, 02.00, ... 12.00, 13.00, ..., 24.00 (= 00.00)

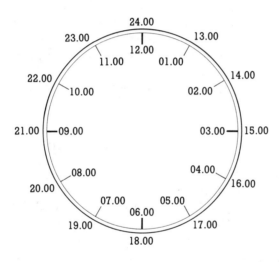

Fig. 8.6

Pupils must be quite clear that this is not decimal notation – the '.' separating hours and minutes is not a decimal point. Other separators can be used, such as h (for hours), e.g. 14 h 35, but official timetables often use no separator – 1435 ; this can cause confusion and, in teaching, it is best to use one.

Printed bus, ship or train timetables may not be readily available and teachers may need to make up some, using local places and services. To start with, these should be very simple, listing only a few places, and not more than two or three services, e.g.

Kinjado	dep. 07.30	11.00	16.45
Nderani	arr. 07.50	11.20	17.10
	dep. 08.05	11.30	17.30
Ijigo	arr. 08.45	12.10	18.15

These provide a basis for questions of many different kinds:

How long does the morning bus wait at Nderani?
Which journey from Nderani to Ijigo is the slowest?
One day the morning bus arrives 26 minutes late at Ijigo – at what time is that?
What is the actual travelling time (i.e. excluding the wait at Nderani) for each journey?

International airline timetables introduce the problem of different time zones. Because the Earth rotates through 360° on its axis every 24 hours, there is a difference of 1 hour of 'sun time' for every 15° of longitude. Every country likes to measure its daily time with the sun roughly overhead at noon, and so the local time is adjusted in relation to Greenwich Mean Time (GMT). GMT is used internationally as a reference time. (At the Royal Observatory at Greenwich, London, the measurement of time was developed to a high degree of accuracy in the first half of the 18th century.)

Here is an example of a timetable of non-stop flights between Ethiopia and Nigeria:

	Addis Ababa	Lagos		Lagos	Addis Ababa
Thu	1000	1250	Fri	0100	0745

It would seem that there is a difference of about four hours in the two journey times, 2 h 50 m east-west and 6 h 45 m west-east! However, the local time in Lagos is one hour ahead of GMT, and Addis Ababa time is three hours ahead of GMT. This means that clocks have to be changed by two hours during the flight. On the journey from Addis to Lagos, they must be put *back* two hours, so the real duration is 2 h 50 m plus two hours. When returning, you need to put your watch *forward* by two hours, so the duration is 6 h 45 m minus two hours. The actual journey times are both about $4\frac{3}{4}$ hours, the average of the apparent times. Obviously, this topic can only be dealt with superficially at primary level.

8.2 SPEED

The concept of time is one of the hardest for young children to understand. Speed, which involves both distance and time, is therefore even harder. Pupils in a rural school may have little experience of road transport or faster means of travel. The following activity introduces speed through pupils' own walking and running; it is a useful exercise for all children.

CLASS ACTIVITY

Choose a measured walking track, 20 m long, on flat level ground. Using a measuring tape (see Section 5.25, p. 104), mark this at 5 m intervals, with every metre marked above 10 m:

Ideally, pupils should work in groups of three. Each group needs a metre strip, graduated in 10 cm intervals and a seconds timer. It is usually possible to hang a seconds pendulum (see Section 8.14) close to the track, and this will serve for all groups. Different groups can be assigned to the activity at different times; if the track is close to the classroom, the teacher can continue to supervise them.
In each group there should be:

a walker, a timer and an observer.

These roles can rotate within the group, so that every pupil walks and has his or her speed measured.
Choose one group to demonstrate to the rest of the class.

1 The walker stands with heels on the zero mark – the observer must check this. The timer prepares the walker to start walking by calling, 'Are you ready? ... Go!'

2 The timer times the walker for 10 seconds. To warn the observer, the timer must call out the last few seconds: ' ... seven ... eight ... nine ... TEN!'

3 The observer needs to stand ready near the 10 m mark, and then to keep alongside the walker so that, when the timer calls, 'TEN!', he can note exactly where the walker's front heel falls.

4 Measure the distance to this heel mark to the nearest 5 cm, using the metre rule.

When these observations and measurements have been made, work out each pupil's walking speed:

a)   In metres per minute
b)   In kilometres per hour.

Note. Pupils should not race, but walk in an easy, natural way.

———————— ◆ ————————

Speed is measured as *distance travelled per unit of time*. It is calculated by dividing the distance travelled by the time taken. This actually gives the *average* speed for the time of the journey, however short.

For most practical, everyday situations we measure speed in *kilometres per hour* (km/h). High speeds may be measured in *metres per second* (m/s). Most people walk steadily at between 4 km/h and 5 km/h. A vehicle speed of 100 km/h is about 28 m/s.

It is helpful to remember that 'per' implies 'divide': kilometres per hour means distance (km) divided by time (h). This relationship between Distance, Time and Speed, is shown by the 'triangle':

To find any of the three formulae connecting the variables, cover up the letter which is to be the subject of the formula:

S   Cover up S: 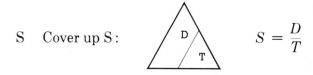 $S = \dfrac{D}{T}$

T   Cover up T: 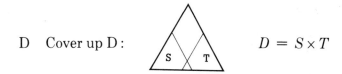 $T = \dfrac{D}{S}$

D   Cover up D: 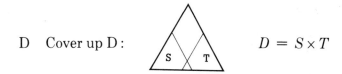 $D = S \times T$

Note. In the triangle, the letters D, S and T are in alphabetical order, reading left-to-right and top-to-bottom.

8.21   Travel graphs

The activity described on p. 181 can be extended in order to produce a simple travel graph of a pupil's walk over ten seconds. For this a group of five observers or markers is needed for each walker and timer.

Each marker needs some small object – a stone or a bottle top – to mark the walker's position. The timer must call out the seconds as the walker walks:

'One ... TWO ... three ... FOUR ... five ... SIX ... seven ... EIGHT ... nine ... TEN !'

stressing every two seconds.

Each of the five markers is allotted a different time – 2, 4, 6, 8 and 10 seconds after the start. During a trial walk, they must space themselves in order along the track, so as to be roughly level with the positions which the walker reaches at their allotted times. They are then ready for the measured walk. The markers watch carefully, and each one marks the position of the walker at his or her allotted time, putting a bottle top or other suitable mark at the spot, as the timer calls the time.

Measure the distance of each of these marks from the zero mark. Record these results carefully:

Time (s)	Distance (m)
0	0
2	
4	
6	
8	
10	

Plot these results on a graph (see Fig. 8.7, overleaf) using a horizontal scale from 0 to 10 seconds and a vertical scale from 0 to 20 metres. The broken line drawn on this graph shows the walker's positions assuming a perfectly steady speed. This speed is, in fact, the average speed for the walk. The points marked 'x' show that the pupil did not, in fact, walk at this constant speed.

Note that on a travel graph, the distance scale records the position of the traveller from some fixed starting point. If a second pupil starts from the other end of the walking track, 20 m from the zero mark, and walks towards the zero, then his graph will slope downwards (see Fig. 8.8a, overleaf).

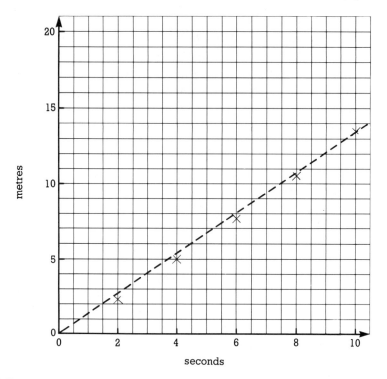

Fig. 8.7

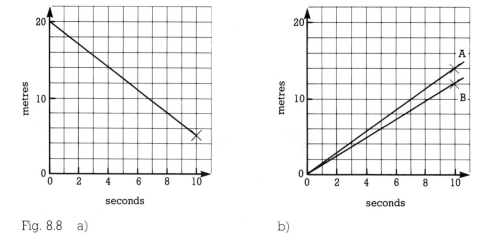

Fig. 8.8   a)   b)

A faster walker covers more ground in the same time. Fig. 8.8b shows the graphs of two walkers, A and B. In the ten seconds, A walks 14 m while B covers only 12 m ; A walks faster than B, and this is shown by the steeper slope of his graph.

When a traveller is stationary his position does not change. The graph in Fig. 8.9 shows the journey of a car which:

a) Sets off from Kinjado at 8 a.m. and travels 40 km to Nderani,
b) Waits at Nderani for 20 minutes,
c) Continues for 30 km to Ijigo, at a slower average speed,
d) Waits at Ijigo for 10 minutes,
e) Returns to Nderani, and then to Kinjado where it arrives at 9.55 a.m.

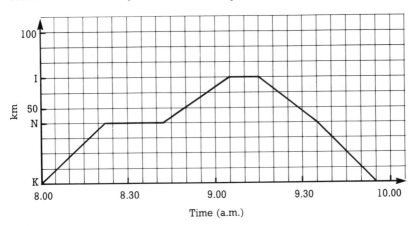

Fig. 8.9

Note that the average speeds on the return journey are faster than on the outward one and, again, the Ijigo – Nderani stage is slower than the Nderani – Kinjado one.

8.3 DIRECT PROPORTION – RATES

Speed is a *rate*, measured as distance *per* unit time. The word 'per' indicates how one measured variable is changing in relation to another. Other examples of rates include:

Cost per unit of mass, e.g. the cost of rice in dollars per kilogram
Wages per hour or day
Density, or mass per unit of volume.

In many cases such a rate may be constant, not changing as the quantities grow in size. We say that such quantities are *proportional* to each other. To put this simply, doubling one quantity leads to doubling the other as well.

A proportional relationship between two quantities is shown, when they are graphed, by a straight line graph through the origin.

8.31 Average speed

The examples and graphs of the last section show that, for a steady speed, distance travelled is proportional to the time taken. For example (see Fig. 8.8b) A travels five times as far in 10 seconds as he travels in 2 seconds. (In practice, of course, his speed varies slightly; his graph would not be a perfect straight line if we could measure his position every tenth of a second and plot 100 points during his 10 second walk.)

8.32 Unit costs

Most marketing of food depends on unit costs. Oranges are sold at so many cents per orange, meat costs so many dollars per kilo, and so on. A graph showing the cost of different quantities of the same food will therefore be a straight line (see Fig. 8.10a).

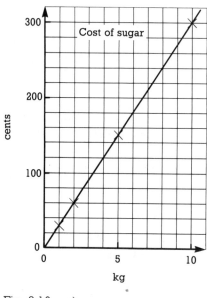

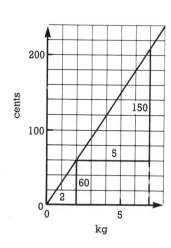

Fig. 8.10   a)   b)

(In practice, traders may give a discount for large amounts, so that the rate per unit is less than it is for smaller amounts.)

When two quantities are proportional, there are different relationships to note. Consider this example:

Mass of sugar (kg)	1	2	5	10	20
Costs (cents)	30	60	150	300	600

1 The ratio cents : kg is the same for each pair of figures :

$$\frac{30}{1} = \frac{60}{2} = \frac{600}{20}$$

In this example, the cost c cents and the mass m kilos are related by the formula

$$c = 30\,m$$

2 The ratio of any pair of masses is the same as the ratio of the corresponding costs, e.g.

$$2 : 10 = 60 : 300$$

3 The straight line graph means that there is an additive relationship between the quantities, e.g.

$$(2 + 5) \text{ kg cost } (60 + 150) \text{ cents}$$

We can see this on the graph in Fig. 8.10b.

8.4 INVERSE PROPORTION

The examples of the last section illustrate what is properly called *direct proportion*. By contrast, with *inverse proportion*, when one quantity decreases the other one increases. Here are two examples :

1 A woman has 60 oranges, and shares them equally between some children. The greater the number of children, the smaller each share is. Six children get ten oranges each, but twelve children would only get five oranges each ; doubling the number of children halves the size of each share. If there are n children, and each one has g oranges,

then $ng = 60$

We can rewrite this formula as :

$$n = \frac{60}{g} \quad \text{or} \quad g = \frac{60}{n}$$

The variables n and g are inversely proportional.

2 Suppose two lorries travel the same journey of 200 km. Lorry A travels at an average speed of 50 km/h and Lorry B averages 40 km/h. The times taken for the journey are 4 h and 5 h respectively ; a faster speed means a shorter journey time. If we call the journey time t hours and the speed s km/h, then $ts = 200$

We can also write this relationship as :

$$t = \frac{200}{s} \quad \text{or} \quad s = \frac{200}{t}$$

The variables t and s are inversely proportional.

8.5 **EXERCISES**

1 The calendar 'moves on' one weekday per year, or two days in a leap year. Work out what day of the week your birthday will fall on in the year 2000.

2 Study the following airline timetables, and work out:
   a) the actual flying times for the journeys (assume they are the same in both directions),
   b) the difference in local time between the two places.

   i)   From NAIROBI to HARARE   From HARARE to NAIROBI
        dep 0915 arr 1105 nonstop   dep 1630 arr 2020 nonstop

   ii) From ADDIS ABABA to BOMBAY   From BOMBAY to ADDIS ABABA
        dep 1245 arr 2015 nonstop   dep 0430 arr 0700 nonstop

3 Fig. 8.11 shows the travel graph of three trains (P, Q, R) on a railway line 100 km long, between two towns A and B. There are three intermediate stations (X, Y, Z) where trains can pass one another.
   i)   Describe the journeys of the three trains.
   ii) Which are the fastest and slowest speeds shown by the graph?

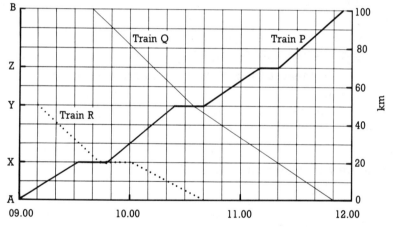

Fig. 8.11

4 Which of the following pairs of quantities are
   a) exactly proportional,
   b) approximately proportional,
   c) not proportional?

   i)   *Mass* of sugar used in a college dining hall: *number* of students in college.
   ii) *Age* of a primary school pupil: *height* of the pupil.
   iii) *Length* of a car journey: *amount* of petrol used on the journey.

iv) *Money paid* for oranges : *number* of oranges bought.

v) *Distance* flown by an aircraft : *time taken* to fly the distance.

vi) *Time taken* to cut the grass in a compound : *number* of labourers employed to cut it.

$$\rule{120pt}{0.4pt} \blacklozenge \rule{120pt}{0.4pt}$$

8.51 Hints and answers

2 i) 2 h 50 m ; 1 hour difference.

ii) 5 h ; $2\frac{1}{2}$ h difference. (India is unusual in differing from GMT by $5\frac{1}{2}$ hours.)

3 i) Train P travels from A to B, and stops at all stations.
Train Q is non-stop from B to A, and passes P while it is waiting at Y.
Train R travels from Y to A and stops at X, where P is waiting for it.

ii) The fastest speed is Q's, from B to Y – about 55 km/h.
(P's from X to Y is about 51 km/h.)
The slowest is R's from X to A – about 30 km/h.

4 a) Only (v), although (iv) is for small numbers (discounts may be given for larger numbers).

b) (i) and (iii)

c) (ii) and (vi) ; (vi) may be, roughly, inversely proportional.

$$\rule{120pt}{0.4pt} \blacklozenge \rule{120pt}{0.4pt}$$

Index